D0983947

The Vision and the Constant Star

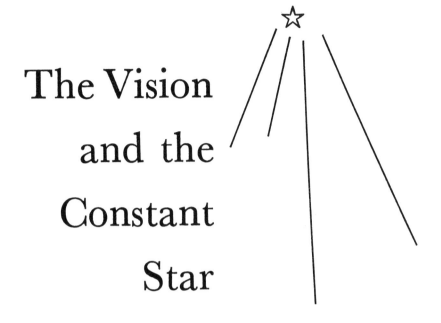

A. H. HOBBS, Ph.D.
University of Pennsylvania, Philadelphia, Pa.
Edited by JOHN HOWLAND SNOW

THE LONG HOUSE, Inc.
1956

COPYRIGHT 1956

The L O N G H O U S E , Inc.
PUBLISHERS

POST OFFICE BOX 1103

NEW YORK 17, N. Y.

Printed in the United States of America

Typography by Eugene M. Ettenberg

$3.50

CONTENTS

FOREWORD

Not far apart, in the *Federalist Papers,* are found two remarkable observations by the two men who exerted more influence than any others in moulding our political institutions. Taken
together, these remarks, by Alexander Hamilton and James Madison, provide the text for the book you are about to enjoy.

Hamilton was pre-eminently a practical statesman. But for a
moment, in No. 11 of the *Federalist,* he becomes a major prophet:
"It belongs to us," says Hamilton there, "to vindicate the honor
of the human race."

That was Vision, from a spokesman for three million scattered
farmers, artisans and small merchants, just beginning to emerge
from colonial status.

Madison had great foresight. He anticipated that the population of the United States would pass two hundred million during the present century. But he knew that if Americans ever
lost their moral fibre this Republic would soon fall in ruins. In
No. 39 of the *Federalist* he reminds us that we "rest all our
political experiments on the capacity of mankind for self-government."

That was the definition of a Constant Star, which today shines
rather dimly for a country with nearly as many government em-
ployes as it had people when Madison told us to beware the
cancer of centralized bureaucracy.

As these complementary quotations suggest, unbounded opti-
mism and deep-rooted humility have ever been the warp and the
woof in the traditional American pattern. Each characteristic de-
rives its strength from the other. The Vision would be mere
bombast if it were not based on a religious conviction of the
dignity of man. The Star has constancy for us only so far as

we are constant in using it as a beacon. Without some guidance higher than immediate desire only the fool can be an optimist.

In this important book Dr. Albert H. Hobbs considers the distortions that now so obviously and grievously mar the symmetry of the American pattern. In sorrow rather than in anger he shows how, in many respects, we have let ill-considered enthusiasms ride roughshod over good judgment. And as we have lost sight of this guiding star, our vision has become ever more materialistic, more debased, less calculated "to vindicate the honor of the human race." With dreadful speed we have followed the *ignis fatuus* of paternalistic government into a quagmire of ever-increasing complications.

Somewhere in this sheeplike stampede that essential "capacity for self-government" has been lost. We talk about saving the world, but all too clearly cannot cope with increasing depravity, debauchery, divorce, drunkenness, delinquency and general damnation at home. More and more people are asking, in bitter disillusionment, how did we ever get this way, and why? Dr. Hobbs has the answer.

It is at bottom the cult of the superficial that has changed us from a people with vision to a visionary people, from hardheaded, God-fearing men and women to loose-living hedonists who above all want somebody else—a dictator would not be amiss—to provide "freedom from fear". Yet, paradoxically, we are of all the so-called "free world" the nation most terrified of communism—simply because we no longer have any faith of our own with which to oppose a hostile doctrine.

Nowhere has this cult of the superficial taken a stronger and more disastrous hold than in what we like to call "social science". Dr. Hobbs, himself a truly scientific thinker, attributes much blame to those who confound science and "scientism"—the meticulous and dispassionate inquiry of the former with the emotional, cause-serving propaganda of the latter. It has been the treason of many self-styled educators to indoctrinate a whole generation with idolatry of the Welfare State.

Some of our socialistic nostrums, especially "social insurance" and "parity prices", are examined in all their sorry detail by Dr. Hobbs in the following pages. Indeed, one of the many virtues of this book is that no point is made without full evidence to sustain it. Yet there is no bitterness in this author's writing. It is not the vision, but only its perversion, that he repudiates. He is no prosecutor of those whose specious humanitarianism has brought us all together into the Slough of Despond. On the contrary, he shows that our only recourse is to struggle out of it as Pilgrim did, by the light of the constant, but now all but neglected, star.

There are, of course, points on which the reader may reasonably disagree with Dr. Hobbs. I myself do not follow the connection he draws between the "classical liberals" and the quasi-Socialists who have usurped the name of liberal today. And if an itemized indictment is to be brought against those Americans who have been most forgetful of the Constant Star, some very prominent conservatives will be well up in the list.

Indeed it is the true liberal—and there are still a lot of them—who will be most interested in Dr. Hobbs' readable and well-reasoned study. For this book has that concern with fundamental values which is of the essence of truly liberal thought. It rises above the dominant interest in the material which often ties conservatives and socialists in an incongruous alliance. On the Right and on the Left there are plenty today who say: "You never had it so good." And, for a time, government spending and deficit financing can keep it so.

That only glosses the underlying decadence that worries Dr. Hobbs, and every thoughtful American with him.

FELIX MORLEY

Gibson Island, Maryland
1956

Part I

Prologue

Preface

AMERICA'S CHALLENGE

A MERICA! Surely, a name to conjure with. Ringing proudly, the sound inspired by this word echoes back through the years to its awakening when a small group of colonists, untrained and yet determined, challenged the mighty empire of Britain.

Foolish was the challenge—it defied all of the arts of warfare; it was contrary to every rule of economics; it did violence to the most elementary canons of reason and of prudence. Yes, it was foolish. But it possessed the unquenchable spirit of independence, the stubborn bravery of pioneers, and the cool courage of a Washington; it surmounted every obstacle, to give birth to a proud Nation.

Struck by these early Colonists, a tocsin reverberated around the world and down through the generations, to us. Hark well to it, that we, now entrusted with its priceless heritage, may pass it on to future ones intact, keeping our personal lives and our Country's course attuned to its ring of honor and of independence, forsaking it not for some siren song played upon an alien instrument.

America! Thunder roars from this word as its sound recalls the gigantic mass of troops and planes and ships gathered at Normandy to storm and shatter the heavy gates of Hitler's *Fortress Europa.*

Large in Europe's skies was written the power of America as her planes by the hundreds, by the thousands, punctuated the

[9]

message of her military might with crashing bombs. The pride and courage of the *Wehrmacht* and the wiles of the legendary Rommel's *Panzers* but served to highlight American audacity as Patton's greased juggernaut thrust into Germany to puncture the myth of her military invincibility.

Proud pages of our military annals attest to the *esprit de corps* of our military élite; to the Marines as they stormed the beaches of Guadalcanal and Tarawa and defiantly raised our Flag on the heights of Iwo Jima.

Not always has victory been ours, but—his men enveloped, half-frozen, during the Battle of the Bulge—the defiant "Nuts" which General McAuliffe hurled back at the German offer of surrender and relief, was typically American. So, too, in the dark early days of the war, with the pride of America's Fleet rusting in the watery grave of Pearl Harbor, the distant Emperor's ships making the Pacific a Japanese lake and his soldiers pouring irresistibly through the Philippines, was General MacArthur's expression of America's indomitable spirit—*I shall return!*

America! Dollars crinkle in the sound of the word—synonymous with wealth. The Land where luxuries are necessities, where the poor live as do princes of many climes, where even in economic adversity we rival the highest prosperity of other lands.

From her seemingly boundless coffers pour foodstuffs, medicines, clothing and machines as gifts to those who receive them with suspicion; who, even in receiving, laud their own spirituality while declaiming the crass and sordid materialism of the giver. Burst from its national bounds, America's wealth pours alike on yesterday's enemy and on today's expedient and reluctant ally—perhaps, too, on tomorrow's foe.

Yes, virtues untold are conjured by this symbol, yet. . . .

America! Corrupt, wallowing in graft and vice, lazy and indulgent. . . . Mecca for crackpot schemes and cults. . . . A land of the brave and home of the free, attesting their bravery by draft-dodging, proving their freedom by mewling pleas for handouts from the Government!

Obsessed with sex but fearful of parenthood, women are girls till their fifties and husbands are often less than men. Hands-down winner, were Olympic competition to include divorce, criminality, racketeering, wastefulness, alcoholism, sexual delinquencies and perversion.

In victory her emissaries of goodwill—all too often arrogant, ill-mannered and undisciplined—spread the message of her virtues by rape, robbery, vainglorious boasting, black-market operations and rank ostentation. Afraid to fight and afraid not to fight. Mightiest of nations, kowtowing to the whim of every other.

[10]

Citadel of capitalism, as proved by loud applause at its abandonment. Center of learning, where Mickey Mouse vies with Mickey Spillane to sharpen the wits of the citizenry. Where the spurious "realism" of vulgarity and lust competes with spurious imagining of spacemen to reap the fruits of long years of education.

America! It is a paradox, and a challenge. It is a challenge to you—and what manner of person are you to meet this challenge?

Youth! You are America's youth. Commencement orators depict you as the hope of the future. With equal warrant you may be its despair. Those who speak of "Youth on the March" may mistake your sloppiness for personality, your blubber for strength, your indifference for tolerance, your glibness for wisdom and your rudeness for independence.

You are more educated than your fathers, more educated than your fellows in other lands. In many ways you were favored from the time of your conception. Your mothers' better diet enabled you to be born bigger and healthier. You encountered fewer dangers of disease, and those you caught were more quickly cured. You are better fed, with a wider variety of food than people ever had in the past. You are taller and heavier and you live appreciably longer than did your ancestors. School offers a greater variety of courses than it did, discipline is relaxed, you study less. After you complete your education you will get a job at high pay. Hours of work are fewer, vacations longer, little pressure is exerted upon you to produce.

You will have an automobile, good housing, radio, television, and whatever other gadgets come along to make life more comfortable, more even and more entertaining. If you lose your job you will receive unemployment compensation, and when you are old the Government promises to pay you a pension. If you are a farmer, the Government will guarantee that you receive minimum prices for your crops.

You Girls! More so even than boys, you have gained in terms of the number of years which you spend attending school. Your chances of getting a job are infinitely greater than were your mothers'. More and more of you will hold a wider variety of jobs for a longer time than did women in the past—and you will call it "pursuing a career". More and more of you will combine your "career" with marriage—primarily to help your husband, of course. Less and less of you will get married, and those of you who do will have fewer children.

All kinds of gadgets—including a dishwiping husband—will lighten your housework. Your bigger feet will seem less large in artfully designed shoes, while lipstick, nail polish, girdles and other artifices and contrivances will enhance your female charms —perhaps at times create them.

You! From your ranks, so fortunately endowed, so well fed, so abundantly educated, there will come more criminals, dope addicts, adulterers and homosexuals than ever before. More of you will spend your days in madhouses. More will get divorced. Ease and relative security will give rise to demands for more ease and more security, and as you are relieved of worries which plagued people in the past you create new worries. You spend all you make, and in the increasingly less likely event that you have enough children (three) to keep the society going, your principal legacy to them is a debt (courtesy of the Government) of some six thousand dollars apiece.

How explain paradoxes embodied in the proud tradition and the widespread indifference, the military might and the spineless equivocation, the unprecedented luxury and the extensive corruption and dissatisfaction which characterize American society and which confront your future?

Challenge always existed in America as, indeed, it has existed continually in all countries.* Individually, the early settlers were repeatedly confronted with starvation, with raging, uncontrolled epidemics, with frightening hostile savages. Collectively, the Colonies faced the question of daring rebellion against a country where many of them were born and which many of them, even in rebellion, loved. Later came the challenge of the Civil War, the first world war and the second, and the hardships and deprivations of the economic depression of the 1930s.

Earlier challenges, however, were different than those of today. The earlier ones were more likely to involve physical action, or clearly defined economic conditions. Today the primary challenge—barring war—is of a moral nature. Moreover, the challenge does not reveal itself as a clear-cut choice between good and evil, each clear and well-defined. Today the challenge is in form a vision—twin-faceted.

It is a vision of personal behavior emancipated from the restraining fetters of traditional moral codes; it is a vision of collective life emancipated from the shackles of economic need.

Furthermore, the vision seems to emanate from science, or from what is believed to be science by many of our people. This seeming-science fortifies the resolve of proponents of the vision; yet those who question it can be readily condemned as unscientific, as reactionary and anti-intellectual. The vision is designed to emancipate the personality of the individual and to guarantee

---

* Arnold Toynbee is widely credited with the recognition of *challenge* as a major force in the rise and fall of civilizations.

the economic security of the group. Collectivism, international-ism, pacifism, equalitarianism, the pleasure-pain calculus of hedonism, and a planned society shine in the focus of the vision. Competition, patriotism, status distinctions, supernaturalism, and traditional moral values are dimmed virtually to extinction by their pale contrast to its rosy glow. The exaltation of short-term secular rationality embodied in the personal vision weighs be-havior on scales for which pleasure or pain are the only counters, while the collective vision of governmentally guaranteed security assumes that the problems of man can be solved by a series of formulas, secular and economic in their nature.

Many desirable features are associated with the life-outlook which I describe as "The Vision". Much pleasure, and a gratify-ing release from responsibilities, are combined with the immoral-ity, criminality, and economic waste and delusion which I call "The Reality". Both the personal and the collective vision appeal to many sincere and thoughtful people, and there are many who will protest that the alternatives I suggest are unduly restrictive of personal behavior and excessively pessimistic in regard to collective endeavors.

There is probably no simple answer to the problems which we face, and surely there is no certain cure. But perhaps a few strands of the subtle interweaving of life's complex pattern in mid-century America can be unravelled for closer examination, by analysis of the vision. I propose no cure-all, no panacea for the ills of society; I offer no sugar pills to make you happy for-evermore. If from this study, however, you glean some small measure of increase in understanding, if it contributes some fiber to weave into stronger resolve to adhere more firmly to your in-dependence as citizens and to your character as persons, then it serves a useful purpose.

Chapter I

The Paradox: A Confused Giant

WHEN persons behave in a way which is at variance with the beliefs which they profess—when they extol charity but refuse to contribute; when they boast of principles but equivocate in practice; when they talk of tolerance but denounce those who fail to agree with *them*—such persons we pity for their self-deception, or label with our scorn as hypocrites. And so it is with nations. Countries which loudly proclaim their love for peace while they cynically practice aggression, and which base their proclaimed democracy upon regimentation, these countries may inspire fear, but seldom will they inspire respect.

As individuals, and as members of American society, we all like to believe that our behavior is consonant with our beliefs. Yet it may be that our present confusion arises, in some measure at least, from practices which indicate a lack of staunch adherence to traditional beliefs. Such practices do not usually involve dramatic, clear-cut defiance, for the beliefs themselves are subtle; our beliefs are sensed rather than precisely defined. They are flexible enough to be adapted to changing conditions, and it may be that our adherence is changed in form rather than weakened in its substance.

The theme presented below, however, is that our practices increasingly depart from our traditional beliefs, and that our continued lip-service adds to the confusion as our behavior continues to belie our belief.

Never, in America, was there a time when everyone believed in exactly the same things with precisely the same degree of feeling. Differences of opinion and differences in the direction and depth of belief always existed, and let us devoutly hope that they always will. At various times, and frequently with an intensity of feeling rarely found today, strong differences of opinion have existed between those who sought separation from the control of England, and the Tories who wished to reconcile the disputes between the Colonies and the mother country; between Antifederalists who believed that the separate Colonies should be only loosely associated into a confederation, and Federalists who were convinced of the absolute necessity for a strong central government. Colonies disputed violently with each other, and religious groups condemned dissenters to damnation. Impassioned controversies arose out of different beliefs about slavery, States-rights, monetary policy, populism, isolationism and a multiplicity of other issues. Yet beneath these differences, and despite the vigor of the disputes, though contentious factions seemed to whip the surface of our history into turbulent froth, there flowed deep strong currents of consistent belief.

We Believed

Specific abuses led John Hancock and his fellow-signers of the Declaration of Independence to appeal to the "Supreme Judge of the world" and solemnly to rely on "the protection of divine Providence" as they pledged their lives, their fortunes and their sacred honor to the cause of Independence. Some practices of "the present King of Great Britain" they believed to be wrong. They objected to quartering large bodies of armed troops on their premises; they protested against protecting such troops from proper punishment for their crimes; cutting off the trade of the colonies; imposing taxes without their consent; and depriving the colonists, in many cases, of trial by jury. A modern sound arises from their protest, hauntingly familiar, that the king was sending "swarms of Officers to harass our people, and eat out their substance." Such abuses they believed to be wrong, yet they did not hold opposite views—pacifism, free trade, abolition of all taxes—as positive beliefs.

Their Declaration of Independence stated as self-evident truth

> . . . that all men are created equal, that they are endowed by their Creator with certain unalienable Rights, that among these are Life, Liberty and the pursuit of Happiness.

What was meant by "equal", and by the right to "Life, Liberty and the pursuit of Happiness", must be interpreted in the light of the facts of the time. Certainly neither the signers of the Declaration nor any appreciable number of people at that time believed that children were equal to adults, that women were equal to men, that Indians were equal to whites, or that indentured servants had the same rights as did citizens of substance and property.

We can say that the Declaration did establish the principle that all men are *equal in the eyes of the law*—in the sense that no man shall have his life taken away or be imprisoned and thus deprived of the liberty to pursue his happiness except by proper legal procedure. Only by distorting the interpretation into a lunatic proclamation can it be held that the Declaration meant to establish that all men are or should be equally tall, equally intelligent, equally swift, or equally rich. To those already possessing liberty, and only to those, it pledged continuance of liberty until found guilty by legal process of an act defined by statute to warrant deprivation of liberty or of life. And certainly the Document was not meant as a guarantee that everyone outside of jail would be happy. The unalienable rights, then, refer to things which should not be done, rather than to positive beliefs.

Perhaps it is desirable that the beliefs which bound America be sensed rather than specifically expressed. The listing which follows suggests some of them:

> We believed that men of noble stature founded this Country and sacrificed their lives for it; that in so doing they entrusted to our hands a glorious tradition, charging us with an obligation to pass it on to future generations intact. We believed that a generation which sullies this tradition betrays its honored trust.

> We believed that this was the best country in the world, and we were proud of our belief.

> We believed that we should worship God and contribute to good works, and that our devotion needed no explanation or apology.

> We believed that it was a privilege to abide by the Ten Commandments, and that honesty was its own reward.

> We believed that decency forbade talk about vulgar things, especially in mixed company, and that to print such things was evidence of a dearth of ability as well as a lack of good taste.

> We believed that women merited respect and courtesy, as did our parents and the aged.

> We believed that competition gave deserving people a chance to succeed and that hard work and ability would win

out despite obstacles; if you failed, chances are it was your own fault. We believed that laziness and improvidence were vices, and that we should be reluctant to accept charity.

Obedience to such beliefs was strictly enjoined upon the young because older and wiser heads were aware of the temptation for youth to call license by the name of liberty; knew how pleasant it is to shun our responsibilities; to absolve the corrupt and to impose undue burdens upon those innocent of any offense, and in so doing to call our equivocation "tolerance" and to call our greed and envy "social justice".

Many such earlier beliefs have been changed, and many are being changed at a rate and to a degree which gives pause for wonder if not for apprehension.

Practice Belies Belief

In this prologue the overall pattern of change will be portrayed within a framework of the major institutions. Later in the book these changes will be described in some detail.

Social Institutions were described by one of the earliest sociologists of America, William Graham Sumner, as involving both a *concept* and a *structure*. The *concept* is an idea, a belief, an ideal as to how the best interests of society will be served within the area of behavior where the institution functions. A *structure* is required to provide the equipment necessary to carry out the purposes of the institution.

Thus the institution of the state in this Country includes in its structure machinery for electing our representatives, rules for making laws and rules for enforcing them. This structure is ordinarily described in some detail in courses in civics. Our concern here is not with the structure but with the concepts upon which the various institutions were founded and the manner in which the practices which we now increasingly permit, and at times even encourage, affect such concepts.

The theme of this outline of institutional change is that while our society was founded on firm principles around which the institutions grew and effectively functioned, now, in increasing degree and at ever faster pace, we not only permit but encourage practices which constitute departures from traditional principles. Though we accept these many practices which deviate from the principles around which we ordered our behavior and created our institutions, we refuse to accept the implications which are inherent in the practices themselves.

We have relinquished our grip upon earlier principles and they are no longer held with a conviction firm enough to provide deep personal satisfaction or social effectiveness. Yet we are reluctant to accept the possible alternatives as positive beliefs around which to readjust our lives or to reorganize our institutions. We still give lip-service to the earlier beliefs; our actual behavior belies our words.

Individual Behavior

Though a few writers have portrayed man as living an idyllic carefree existence in a state of nature, roaming gaily through primitive forests and unrestrained in his expression, such descriptions arise solely out of the writer's own romantic imagination and have no significant relation to what is known about actual primitive conditions. Man, by virtue of his very limitations in a struggle for survival with other animals, had to band together into groups. Human behavior in even the most primitive groups is severely restricted; life is regulated by taboos, codes, superstitions and tribal precepts. Though such primitive controls on behavior are unwritten, though they may differ widely from group to group, though they may arise out of superstition and be perpetuated by ignorance, though they may be in shocking contrast to the regulations which are imposed upon the members of civilized societies, they do operate to prescribe types of permissible behavior and to prohibit behavior which is believed to be harmful.

In a civilized society the rules for behavior are written as well as verbal; and to a much greater degree than is true in primitive groups, they have an appreciable degree of consistency in that they are centered around a fairly coherent philosophy of life.

Religion is the institution from which arise most of our basic codes of conduct. The institution of religion serves a vital societal purpose by binding together in a spiritual sense the members of the society. For individual members of the society, religion serves this fundamental purpose by establishing a type of continuity to life which could be derived from no other source. Across a vast continent, among widely differing areas and peoples, down through successive generations which witnessed profound changes in the material aspects of life, religion provided a spiritual continuity.

It was the source from which people derived meaning for their lives; it provided not only solace in time of trouble but, much more importantly, contributed a consistent spiritual framework which transcended adversity and which reconciled the many inconsistencies in the people's secular experience. It was a source to which people looked for ultimate and permanent values on which their codes of conduct could be based.

Monotheism, the worship of a single spiritual God, was the belief upon which the institution of religion was established in our Country. For the vast majority of our people the type of monotheism was Christianity, and it was from the moral codes associated with Christianity that we obtained rules which governed the more important aspects of our behavior. Such rules were looked upon as emanating from divine revelation, or at least as being spiritual manifestations. They were thought of as being permanent and inviolable.

In his first inaugural address (1801) Thomas Jefferson expressed the role of religion as a guide to human behavior as

> . . . enlightened by a benign religion, professed, indeed, and practiced in various forms, yet all of them inculcating honesty, truth, temperance, gratitude, and the love of man; acknowledging and adoring an overruling Providence, which by all its dispensations proves that it delights in the happiness of man here and his greater happiness hereafter.

Washington, in his first inaugural address (1789) warned

> . . . that the propitious smiles of Heaven can never be expected on a nation that disregards the eternal rules of order and right which Heaven itself has ordained . . .

Though most of us continue to give lip-service to the spiritual beliefs associated with religion, in practice we turn more and more to secular sources for guidance. Increasingly, we seek the advice and read the books of psychiatrists, psychoanalysts and mental hygienists, not only to solve specific emotional problems but for an explanation of the mainsprings of behavior. Marriage counsellors and sex education programs are turned to for advice by increasing numbers of people. Surprisingly, and of vital significance in this trend which seeks secular rather than spiritual interpretations, many of the clergy not only condone the practice but actually (as will be described later) laud and recommend it. There are those among the clergy who, rather than deplore and restrain such trends, seek the vanguard in this secular movement.

Yet we will not accept any of the clear-cut opposites to spiritual monotheism as a source from which to derive the core of meaning to life and individual behavior. Only a few accept atheism and flatly disavow divine influence in human affairs, and rarely exceptional are the agnostics—those who are afraid to disbelieve, as they are afraid to believe. Few bluntly advocate a completely secular interpretation of all human behavior even though they laud tendencies in this direction as being rational. Thus we still give lip-service and go through rituals which seem to conform to earlier religious belief, and we are not ready enough or courageous enough or perhaps frantic enough to accept the clear alternatives to that belief.

The religious institution thus fails to function as effectively as it did in the past to serve as a common source from which life's ultimate purposes and rules can be derived.

Education is an institution designed to provide formal training so that children may learn the history and traditions of the society; place current events within a framework larger than that of their immediate interests or personal concerns, and raise their interpretations to a higher level than that conveyed by the politics and passions of the moment. Life in a civilized society requires special skills such as mathematics and language, which are acquired in the educational process, but the overall purpose is to produce decent, law-abiding, responsible citizens who will contribute, each within the limits of his ability and according to the bent of his talent, to the welfare and development of the society.

In earlier days the belief was sometimes expressed that a principal purpose of education was to develop Christian ladies and gentlemen. This ideal was not generally regarded in a narrow sectarian sense, but as one applying to all religious groups, conveying the notion of a need to combine good manners and good works with religious belief. Rightly or wrongly, it was believed that traditions of honesty, independence and fair play, proper manners and the desirability of adhering to a firm moral code could be instilled through competition involving discipline and drill. Beneath the discipline and drill, underlying the spelling bees, the mental arithmetic tests, the repetition of the alphabet and of arithmetic tables, seemed to be a belief that specific skills and particular facts were less important than the manner in which they were learned.

Ideally, the exemplary behavior of the teacher was to be coupled with strict but just punishment, while direct learning from maxims dealing with honesty, courtesy, character and courage was combined with indirect lessons instilled through discipline and drill. An extreme expression of the beliefs which seemed to underlie the process was to the effect that it didn't matter what was taught, so long as it was unpleasant!

Wide variations now exist in educational techniques and, particularly in cities, many practices are at sharp variance with the type of belief which dominated our educational institutions during earlier times. Development of the personality seems, at least in some schools, to be more stressed than development of character. Passing events, the transient disputes of the present, seem to be emphasized almost to the exclusion of traditions of the past. Cooperation is emphasized more than competition; adjustment more than integrity. Facts assume equal or higher status than principles. Educational processes are increasingly geared to the interests of children rather than to the values of society. Drill is shunned with repugnance and discipline is condescendingly referred to as signifying a failure to arouse proper interest. With exaggeration, it might be said that now it does not matter what is taught, nor how, so long as it is pleasant!

Yet no appreciable group of educators, much less of parents, would uphold as a positive ideal an education which merely supplies pupils with facts and ignores principles, which entertains rather than trains, which develops personality to the point where pupils become self-centered, show-off brats with little regard for their responsibilities to society. Marked changes seem to indicate that education, like religion, is no longer characterized by sufficiently strong adherence to earlier beliefs to enable the institution to function effectively. Yet here too there is reluctance to accept alternative notions (personal rationality but social irresponsibility, current factual knowledge without binding principles) as positive belief.

Family Life

In its simplest essentials the family institution serves its primary societal function, that of perpetuating the group, by producing children and by providing them with informal training. Though some members of a few groups within the society once had group approval when they engaged in plural marriage, it was generally and firmly believed that the institution of the family could best fulfill its purpose within a framework of strict permanent monogamy. Marriages were entered into solemnly, without any mental reservations concerning the injunction: "Till death do us part." Divorce was exceedingly rare, and in the few cases where it did occur, social stigma was attached to the divorced person, particularly to divorced women.

The strong spiritual tone associated with marriage found expression in sayings such as "Marriages are made in Heaven", and "Let no man put asunder those whom God has joined together". Marriage was looked upon as a social responsibility, as an obligation of adulthood. Failure to meet the obligation to marry resulted in social reaction which ranged from amusement to scorn. Again, the reaction was stronger against women who failed to fulfill the obligation than it was toward men. Married couples without children were looked upon askance.

Among other things, the family was a center of religious life, with family prayers, grace at mealtimes, and hymn-singing the rule in homes where the family Bible was so integral a part of life that its entries of births, deaths, property settlements and wills had complete legal validity.

Family life was patriarchal, with the husband possessing many rights and privileges which the wife was denied. If questions arose as to the authority within the home, custom, law and social pressures usually decreed that the wife was subordinate to her husband, as were children to the father. Wives were to center their thoughts and their activities upon bearing and raising children and upon managing the household. Activities outside this sphere were limited to religion, to interest in charities, and to a few permissable hobbies—none of which were to interfere with the primary responsibilities of helpmeet, mother and manager of the household.

Moral standards were strict, and those for women were appreciably more rigid and demanding than those for men. A double standard existed, wherein men could engage in some forms of behavior which women could not. Men could drink in public, smoke and swear without arousing scorn or wrath. Some condemnation was directed at men who engaged in sexual relations prior to marriage, but not nearly so much nor so severe as that directed at women.

Associated with such beliefs about marriage and the family was a conviction that sexual matters were not to be discussed publicly, especially in mixed company. Sex was veiled in an atmosphere of mystery.

Beneath this pattern was a belief that men and women were essentially different in their interests and in their abilities, and that societal welfare would be served most effectively through marital arrangements in which the relationships were established upon an equitable, rather than on an equal, basis. As at least partial compensation for the more demanding and more rigid code to which they were required to conform, women received special treatment. Women were accorded courtesies and considerations by virtue of their sex, and motherhood was looked upon with a respect which sometimes verged upon veneration.

Though we still give lip-service to permanent monogamy, we permit more and more exceptions. Hundreds of thousands of divorces granted each year attest to the fact that our practices constitute a significant departure from a former belief in permanent monogamy. Since most people marry again after they are divorced, it might almost be said that we favor *consecutive* monogamy; that we now believe a man should marry only one woman at a time!

Spiritual aspects are being dissolved from their association with marriage, and the relationship is increasingly viewed as a secular arrangement which has as its central purpose "the adjustment of two personalities". Whether to marry and, once married, whether to have children, is looked upon as a matter of individual preference rather than as a social responsibility. Derision, once directed at the "old maid", is now replaced with the respectful, sometimes envious, designation "career woman", or by the paradoxical expression "bachelor girl". Both in number and as a percentage of all marriages, childless marriages increase, while in some places at least couples with more than four children are looked upon with amused condescension. Little or no stigma attaches to divorced persons.

Rights and privileges for wives and children increase and are coupled with a decrease in the rights and privileges of husbands to weaken the partriarchal structure of the family. More than one-third of the gainfully employed persons in the United States are now women, and of these more than half—over ten million—are married women. In practice it becomes increasingly common for women to continue to work ("to pursue a career") after marriage.

Moral standards decline precipitously, and within the pattern of general and rapid decline; the standards of women, though still somewhat more restrictive, descend relatively more rapidly than those of men. Courses in training for marriage become increasingly common, with sexual matters receiving prominent attention. Such courses are buttressed by books and articles in which sexual matters are freely discussed. Some restraints still exist, but the veils of mystery are rapidly being stripped away in a frantic Salome's dance. As women engage in occupations alongside men, as they smoke and swear and lower their standards till they approach those of men; as their femininity is transformed into good-fellow companionship; as their greater variety of experiences robs them of capacity for shock and indignant revulsion; as they demand equality rather than equity, the special treatment—the courtesies and chivalry formerly accorded them—gradually fades away.

Yet the alternatives to permanent monogamy are not looked upon as positive and desirable goals. We do not actively recommend bigamy or any other form of multiple marriage, nor do we generally advocate divorce, advising our children to "marry early and often". We do not openly advocate immorality for its own sake. Though recommendations for sexual license are made, as in the works of Professor Kinsey and several others, they are still cloaked in the somber garments of "science" and are presented as a means for attaining marital adjustment rather than as desirable goals in themselves. With marriage and family relationships we are also at a point in our social history where we refuse to hold fast to earlier beliefs around which the institutions developed, where our practices permit and even encourage increasing exceptions, but we are not willing to accept the implications of our behavior as positive and desirable goals for ourselves or for society. Many, of course, still honor tradition.

The State and the Economy

Changes in relation to the beliefs on which the institutions of the state and the economy were founded are outlined together because such changes have been closely intertwined for a number of decades.

In simplest terms, the fundamental purpose of the state is to preserve order within the society, to assure that formal regulations in the form of laws are established and enforced. Such laws may be many and rigid, as they are under a tyranny or under a dictatorship, but in America it was believed that citizens should retain a maximum of freedom and that governmental regulation should be kept to the absolute minimum necessary for the preservation of order.

Such limited and specifically enumerated powers as were delegated to the Federal Government included those necessary to levy and collect taxes and duties, to borrow money, to regulate foreign and interstate commerce, to establish uniform rules of naturalization and bankruptcy, to coin money and regulate its value, to fix standards of weights and measures, to punish counterfeiters, to establish a postal system, to issue patents for the protection of inventors, to establish a federal system of courts, punish piracy, declare war, raise and support an army and navy, and to call forth the militia to suppress insurrection or to repel invasion. Thus the Constitution limited the powers of the Federal Government to those areas specifically enumerated, reserving (in the Tenth Amendment) all other powers ". . . to the States respectively, or to the people."

This principle of strict limitation of powers was confirmed throughout the years by the Supreme Court of the Nation, and was most succinctly expressed by Thomas Jefferson at his first inaugural in 1801. President Jefferson attributed the wellbeing of the Republic to its separation from entanglement in the affairs of Europe, to its broad expanse and natural wealth, to a spirit of independence which led men to judge others by worth rather than by birth, to the influence of religion, and to

> . . . a wise and frugal Government, which shall restrain men from injuring one another, shall leave them otherwise free to regulate their own pursuits of industry and improvement, and shall not take from the mouth of labor the bread it has

earned. This is the sum of good government, and this is necessary to close the circle of our felicities.

Later, expressing his opinion on the constitutionality of a national bank, Jefferson contended that for Congress to expand beyond the limits set upon its powers by the Constitution would be

> ... to take possession of a boundless field of power, no longer susceptible of any definition.

As for the "Welfare Clause", which in recent years has been interpreted as granting virtually unlimited power for Congress to provide for the welfare not only of the Union, but also for special groups within the Union, Jefferson stressed:

> Congress are not to lay taxes *ad libitum, for any purpose they please;* but only *to pay the debts, or provide for the welfare, of the Union.* In like manner, they are not *to do anything they please,* to provide for the general welfare, but only *to lay taxes* for that purpose. To consider the latter phrase, not as describing the purpose of the first, but as giving a distinct and independent power to do any act they please which might be for the good of the Union, would render all the preceding and subsequent enumerations of power completely useless. It would reduce the whole instrument to a single phrase — that of instituting a Congress with power to do whatever would be for the good of the United States; and, as they would be the sole judges of the good or evil, it would be also a power to do whatever evil they pleased.*

Correctly or incorrectly, for good or for bad, our Government was developed around a firm belief that its powers should be strictly limited, reserving a maximum of sovereignty to the separate States and of freedom to the individual citizens. While we still pay our verbal respects to the principle of freedom from government control, few of us in practice adhere firmly to the principle of rigidly limited government.

Businessmen as well as laborers, corporations as well as unions, farmers and city dwellers, not only accept but, with growing frequency, demand increasing governmental intervention, though they know that to accept it means inevitable regulations, an inescapable curtailment of freedom.

Some seven hundred pages are required in the *United States Government Organization Manual 1953-4* merely to give an outline of the various bureaus, agencies and divisions of the Federal Government. Under the executive branch alone, in addition

---

* The italics are in the original document.

to the ten major departments (State, Treasury, Defense, Justice, Post Office, Interior, Agriculture, Commerce, Labor, and the Department of Health, Education and Welfare) the following independent offices and establishments operate:

Atomic Energy Commission
Civil Aeronautics Board
Defense Materials Procurement
 Agency
Defense Transport Administration
District of Columbia
Export-Import Bank of Washington
Federal Civil Defense Administration
Federal Communications Commission
Federal Deposit Insurance Corporation
Federal Mediation and Conciliation
 Service
Federal Power Commission
Federal Reserve System
Federal Trade Commission
General Services Administration
Housing and Home Finance Agency
Interstate Commerce Commission

Mutual Security Agency
National Advisory Committee for
 Aeronautics
National Labor Relations Board
National Mediation Board
National Science Foundation
Railroad Retirement Board
Reconstruction Finance Corporation
Securities and Exchange Commission
Selective Service System
Small Defense Plants Administration
Smithsonian Institution
Tax Court of the United States
Tennessee Valley Authority
United States Civil Service
 Commission
United States Tariff Commission
Veterans' Administration

Under each of these commissions, corporations, agencies, boards, services, foundations and administrations there are dozens of divisions, offices and bureaus to form the wondrous complexity which now is government.

The economic institution develops and functions for the primary purpose of supplying material needs and wants within the society. Our earlier belief was that such purposes could best be fulfilled by a system of private enterprise and capitalism. High esteem was accorded to individual initiative, thrift and personal responsibility. Now, however, more and more groups, each with its own interests, insist that the government play an increasingly active role to provide them with economic ends, rather than remain a referee to insure that fair means are employed for each to attain his own. Most of the fields into which the government has spread are primarily economic, and practices associated with the Wages and Hours Act, Social Security Act, Taft-Hartley Act, the Parity Program, Fair Trade Practices Act, the Federal Housing Programs and a vast conglomerate of other legislation indicate that in the economic area also our practices reflect a lack of vigorous adherence to earlier beliefs.

Communists promote their program in the United States, and the Socialist Party has on occasion secured a fairly large third-party vote, while a substantial segment of the population shows no real objection to measures which are included under the term "Welfare State". Yet only a small minority upholds as a positive ideal a regimented economy in which the state exercises minute control over individual behavior. While we accept practices which point in the direction of increasing economic regulation, we still voice distrust and distaste for governmental regimentation.

Most people would laud at least some of the changes which have taken place in relation to the major institutions of the society, and it is not my purpose to contend that none of them should take place nor that they constitute unmitigated evil. As yet, however, we have failed to crystallize our hopes and ideals around positive alternatives, and we find ourselves in a welter of indecision, afraid to adhere rigorously to the old, too timid to orient ourselves to the new.

What I have tried so far to emphasize is that we seem to be in a sort of Sargasso Sea so far as many of our most important beliefs are concerned. No longer do we hold fast to earlier beliefs around which our major institutions were established and through which for so long they functioned. The degree of the weakening of our beliefs seems amply attested by the multitude of practices which are at variance with them. Perhaps, without being consciously aware of the process, we are even now crystallizing our institutions around some new set of beliefs. Such beliefs, though as yet not clearly formulated, may be as effective as were the older ones, possibly more effective, perhaps less effective. Another possibility, unpleasant but real, is that we are in a state of aimless drift which might result in the disintegration of the society as we know it; where we may be easily redirected by some strong but alien belief.

Changes such as these, vital in importance and perhaps crucial to the very existence of the society, cannot be measured accurately nor scientifically, nor can anyone say with certainty what they bode for the future.

This very unpredictability itself is part of the challenge of the times.

Interwoven Problems

We tend to think of our personal behavior as being one thing, our marital relationships another, and we would jeer at an assertion that the Commodity Credit Corporation is related to either. Certainly, in their details, there is much difference between our personal acts, our marriage vows, and conditions in the state and economic systems; yet, in some measure at least, the seemingly separate beliefs and the acts arising from such beliefs may be interrelated.

[27]

Thirty years ago, Irving Babbitt (in *Democracy and Leadership*, a book so remarkably predictive of the course of events and so acutely perceptive of the central problems of republican government that it was republished in 1954) analyzed this interrelation between seemingly separate problems:

> When studied with any degree of thoroughness, the economic problem will be found to run into the political problem, the political problem in turn into the philosophical problem, and the philosophical problem itself to be almost indissolubly bound up at last with the religious problem.
>
> *(Introd., p.i)*

More recently, Robin M. Williams, Jr., in his *American Society*, gives a number of examples of the manner in which efforts to cope with problems in one area of behavior influence other areas. Professor Williams describes how a measure designed to reduce a health hazard (the requirement that milk be pasteurized) led to a significant economic development, the growth of giant milk distributing firms; and how building codes, established primarily to protect health, brought about significant economic changes among building contractors and craft unions.

So common that we ordinarily ignore its implications is the fact that much economic activity is inextricably associated with personal behavior and the beliefs which govern it, and faith. Paper currency has value only because of an assumption of integrity on the part of the Government. Economic contracts, stocks and bonds, insurance contracts and contributions to Social Security are all based upon a large element of belief and faith.

James Bryce (*Modern Democracies*, 1921) described civil liberty as the exemption of the citizen from control in respect to his person and property; individual liberty as exemption from control in matters which do not so plainly affect the welfare of the whole community as to render control necessary. He then raised the question as to whether laws forbidding the use of intoxicants, or laws limiting the hours during which a man may work, or laws making vaccination compulsory, or laws fixing a minimum wage, infringe civil liberty or infringe individual liberty.

Neither in their individual expression nor in their social effects do our beliefs restrict their influence to separate and limited areas which can be considered completely independent one from another. Rather, it seems, fuller understanding of both our traditions and our current situation can be gained by viewing them as influenced by sets of beliefs which alike affect our individual behavior, our marital relations, our economic outlook and even, to appreciable degree, our form of government. We tend to ignore this interrelation between practices on the individual level, the marital level, the economic level, and in government because, for one thing, technological developments obscure changes which take place in the culture, and for another, we have been exposed to a one-sided interpretation of cultural development.

In his book, *Society*, R. M. MacIver makes a useful distinction by emphasizing several differences between civilization and culture. Professor MacIver points out that a typewriter is part of civilization while the book or play written by its use is part of the culture. Perhaps the distinction is made clearer if we think in terms of differences between *technology* and culture. A typewriter or a printing press is part of the technology, as would be radios, airplanes, television sets and automobiles. The manner in which these are used, however, depends upon the cultural values. Typewriters and printing presses may be used to create and spread communist propaganda, crass vulgarity, scientific works, or religious publications. Communists or capitalists, Catholics or Protestants, militarists or pacifists, the devout or the atheistic alike can employ the instruments of technological development. The purpose in their use, however, would be a measure of the cultural values, of the nature and quality of their beliefs. Automobiles may be used as ambulances on errands of mercy or as get-away vehicles for bank robbers. They can be used for trips which knit a family together in mutual enjoyment of the wonders of nature, or as coffins for those who would prove their superiority by demonstrating that they can press a gas pedal.

Generally, the instruments of technology are devices through which values—the beliefs and attitudes which constitute the essence of the culture—can find expression. While we all have access to the products of technology, Professor MacIver contends that what we acquire from the culture depends upon what we are, that we acquire culture selectively, as we are worthy or unworthy. Unlike technology, which accumulates almost automatically, culture must be won anew by each generation.

Technological developments are awesomely impressive, and when we view society in their terms we cannot but pronounce its success. But this impressive technology may lead us to overlook what is actually more basic, the purpose for which it is created; it may lead us to minimize changes which take place in the culture which the technology serves.

Coupled with our propensity to gauge our condition in terms of technological developments from which we derive justifiable pride, have we not been led by some scholars to examine our traditions and to view our lives through the small end of a telescope which focuses our gaze upon a narrow, segmental, and secular field?

An entire generation of the most influential historians, led by

Professor Charles A. Beard, thus fostered an interpretation of our Constitution and our history solely or primarily in terms of economic interests. The influence of this and similar doctrines will be described in "The Source". For the present, suffice it to indicate that our admiration for technological devices has very often been coupled with a narrow, segmental and secular view to obscure the influence of beliefs and ideals, both in an interpretation of our history and in a description of contemporary problems and performance.

The theme here presented is that fundamentally our culture must be judged, and that it will succeed or fail, in terms of individual beliefs and ideals. Such beliefs must be more than empty phrases which our behavior belies; they must flow from a depth of conviction which constitutes a wellspring from which our institutions can draw continuous sustenance.

At the very outset of our history as a Nation, Washington, in delivering his first inaugural address, stated that

> ... the foundation of our national policy will be laid in the pure and immutable principles of private morality ...

Similar expression is found in *Puritanism and Democracy,* wherein Professor Ralph Barton Perry states:

> However great the natural ... or historical importance of society, it may still be true that the final values of life begin and end with individuals, and with the states or acts of individuals, such as desire, hope, love ...   *(P. 440)*

To deny the role of individual beliefs, to negate them in practice not only in our personal behavior but in relation to family life, to economic pursuits, and to governmental affairs—to be blinded by the glister of shiny technological devices—may lead to the condition portrayed by Herman Melville:

> In glut of all material arts
> A civic barbarism may be:
> Man disennobled—brutalized
> By popular science—atheized
> Into a smatterer ...

As we renounce our heritage we blame our personal dissatisfaction and our public confusion on the circumstances in which we find ourselves, and perhaps in so doing we are like the youth who murdered his parents and then begged the court for mercy because he was an orphan.

Thus the paradoxes are dramatized and our earlier beliefs contrasted with our present behavior.

What, then, do we seek? This question is arranged in two main sections: The first, "The Personal Quest: Emancipation." This section deals with individual and marital behavior in terms of changing beliefs and practices. The second part, "The Collective Quest: Security", interprets in similar fashion economic and governmental events.

Each section is divided into four parts: "The Vision", which describes the nature of the newer beliefs which seem to be replacing the older; "The Source", which describes the origin of the newer beliefs and the manner in which they are spread; "The Reality", which stresses the influence of the newer beliefs upon individual behavior and upon social conditions, and portrays some of the fallacies inherent in them; and fourth, "The Maxims", in which an attempt is made to affirm fundamental principles which apply to individual behavior and to social conditions.

An epilogue, "The Recourse", recommends some principles which, if incorporated into our private lives and applied to our public affairs, might constitute ballast against capricious waves of expediency which now toss us about; might serve as guidance toward some sound direction to our aimless drift.

Let me remind the reader that in none of this is there a one-way ticket to Utopia; there is no neatly etched blueprint of the future, no panacea for perpetual pleasure on this earth. Here is an interpretation and an analysis. And while some may applaud its perceptiveness, others, I am sure, will denounce its limitations. While some may approve the principles recommended, others, and perhaps with equal warrant, will decry them as outmoded dogma. None of these—neither applause nor denunciation, neither approval nor depreciation—is central to the purpose of this essay. This is an effort to arouse readers to an awareness of the challenge of America, to bestir their intelligence in regard to the problems, to sharpen their feelings in order to cut into the maze of current contradictions.

We awake; we bestir—else we continue powerful above all nations, but in our purposelessness easy prey to winds of discord, *A Confused Giant*, or, as more than a century ago Horace Mann predicted:

> . . . [if] a republic be devoid of intelligence, it will only the more closely resemble an obscene giant . . . whose brain has been developed only in the region of the appetites and passions, and not in the organs of reason and conscience. . . . Such a republic, with all its noble capacities for beneficence, will rush with the speed of a whirlwind to an ignominious end.

Part II

The Personal Quest: Emancipation

Chapter II

The Vision: Emancipation

O N HIS farm, alone and ill, Whittaker Chambers
—former Communist, former courier for one
of several Soviet espionage rings which operated in the highest
echelons of our Government—wrote *Witness* as a testament to
the world and to his children. His "Foreword in the Form of a
Letter to My Children" attempted to explain why he, so excep-
tionally endowed with intelligence and so extremely sensitive to
personal evil and to social injustice, became a communist agent.

Without underestimating the importance of economic problems
and the real threat of nuclear bombing, the question he raises—
Why were well-educated, intelligent, sensitive Americans so gul-
lible that they became secret emissaries of a brutal and cynical
international conspiracy. . . . Why did they, in lesser degree of
guilt but in much greater numbers, espouse doctrines so alien to
the heritage of their Land?—is central to the issue of America's
challenge.

Chambers describes the motivation for such behavior in terms
of a vision and a conviction.

"It is necessary to change the world" constitutes, according to
Chambers, the conviction which is the tie that binds communists
"across the frontiers of nations, across barriers of language and
differences of class and education, in defiance of religion, morality, truth, law, honor, the weaknesses of the body and the irreso-
lutions of the mind, even unto death."

This conviction was expressed also by Klaus Fuchs, found guilty of passing secret information on atom bombs to Soviet agents. Fuchs was asked how, knowing of the slave labor and oppression in the U.S.S.R., he could engage in espionage, and he answered:

> I came to a point where I knew that I disapproved of many actions of the Russian Government and of the Communist party, and I still believed that they could build a new world and that one day I would take part in it, and that on that day I would also have to stand up and say to them that there are things which they are doing wrongly.

In this queer assertion Fuchs illustrated how deeply possessed a person can become with the conviction that it is necessary to change the world; but for our purposes those who have the conviction in more moderate, yet sincere, form are far more significant than communist spies.

A good expression of this type of conviction is found in one of the volumes of the House Committee on Un-American Activities[1] wherein a college graduate describes why he became interested in communism while a student and tells about the type of student who, according to his experience, was most likely to accept the communist line and to support communist-front organizations:

> That young person who is serious-minded, who is interested in the problems of the world and doing something about them—they are the material that the Communists take and develop. The skillful Communist recruiter can make such a picture for this person of this glittering future, he can show them exactly how to go about creating; he can prove to them, after he has gotten them receptive, that the people of the Soviet Union and China are marching toward this glorious future. He can do all these things with those receptive young minds, and if those young people do not have a firm foundation of belief in God and in their church, the Communists will succeed with those people.
>
> . . . there are none of my acquaintances who evidenced the same type of social conscience and perplexity about life and the meaning of life and wish to do something about it to create this better world—but there were none of those people who had a sure belief in God and tied themselves to the church who were recruited by us. We could not recruit them.   (P. 3322)

Many things are wrong in this world and with the America we live in, and those who feel deeply that the world, or the Country, must be changed are to be lauded rather than condemned. Yet

---

NOTE:—Numbered references will be found listed on page 186.

the conviction that the world must be changed is, as Mr. Chambers points out, founded on a vision, a vision, moreover, of complete secular supremacy:

It is the vision of man's mind displacing God as the creative intelligence of the world. It is the vision of man's liberated mind, by the sole force of its rational intelligence, redirecting man's destiny and reorganizing man's life and the world. *(P. 9)*

It is a vision of emancipation. It is a vision of release not only from limitations imposed by supernatural belief but also of escape from the restrictive influence of customs and tradition. It is an exaltation of secular rationality, of an intellect loosed from both supernatural and historical ties and free to examine personal and social problems from what seems to be a new and promising perspective. It has been described as *individuation,* "the emergence of the individual relatively released from the bindingness of custom as custom and free to think and act for himself, free to adjust to reality as it exists rather than to preconceptions of it which may be crystallized in the folkways, mores, and institutions of his group."

Words which describe the vision have a brave new ring and the appeal is strong, so strong as to be almost irresistible to those who are adrift, those with no firm allegiance either to their religion or to their country's tradition, and to those who believe that their superior intellect should accord them status higher than the one they hold. Some who become entranced with the vision fall prey to communist dogma which cloaks its own political purpose within similar fine phrases. Such are numerically few, and by far the larger number of those who are attracted by it are respectable humanitarian people who sincerely believe that the vision provides them with a new and a true light for our mutual problems. They believe that the vision enables them to examine important issues with no interference from preconceptions. And, while serious doubt regarding such freedom from bias may be raised, little doubt exists as to their sincerity.

Education and The Vision

The educational process was to be changed—to be child-centered, not subject-centered. To teach the child, not the subject, was another ideal. Teachers were to be guided by the interests of their pupils rather than by rigid demands of a curriculum. Pupils were to be taught to make a real-life adjustment to modern conditions of living rather than to be indoctrinated with unrealistic abstractions and outmoded traditions. They were to be trained to think for themselves, not to rely upon rote memory. School work was to be evaluated in terms of the natural ability of the pupil rather than in terms of artificial, abstract standards such as grades. Emphasis was to be placed upon the degree of creativity displayed rather than upon the amount of work accomplished.

To develop the whole personality, a well-rounded, adjusted personality with an emancipated mind—a mind which will enable the pupils to act in accordance with rational conclusions—this fine-sounding ideal is one of the expressions of the vision.

In the field of education the vision found expression through what was first called the "activity program", then came to be known as "progressive education", and now generally is called the "modern teaching method." Extracting from issues of the official journal of the Progressive Education Association from 1925 through 1948, a graduate student of mine, Mary Ann Gehres, found that such expressions characterized the progressive doctrine. Desirability of cooperation rather than competition was stressed, for example, by an educationist who directed his fellows that

> We must explain to [the pupils] the futility of individual ambition—its failure to provide emotional satisfactions and to bring about the development of a new and better world.[2]

Part of the vision was a strong belief in the necessity to persuade students to think in terms of internationalism rather than in terms of nationalism, expressed by one writer in this way:

> Citizenship is the relation of the individual to the group, whether conceived in its pure political sense or in its wider application to human interrelations in all phases of life and without reference to national boundaries.[3]

Other educationists, enamored of the international aspects of the vision, were more extreme, and more explicit:

> We shall criticize our projects and curriculum on the basis of their social values, encouraging our more mature students to study and identify themselves with vital world movements, including, of course, the Russian experiment.[4]

Representative Paul W. Shafer and John Howland Snow have provided the best single and short description of the development of this movement in education in their book *The Turning of the Tides*.[5] In their description of efforts to promote an international outlook, they cite the manner in which educationists refer to patriotic sentiments as "the poisoned air of nationalism", "the poison of aggressive nationalism", "diseased nationalisms", "jingoism", and in similar terms.

[35]

In education, the vision at first found expression through sentiments relating to the emancipation of children, but before long efforts to "change the world" outweighed those designed to emancipate their minds. Efforts to change American society through education began with moderate and idealistic attempts to lead children to understand certain abuses, but these efforts soon developed into the very type of indoctrination which previously had been so severely condemned. Then, of course, indoctrination, which had been unnecessary and bad, became necessary and good. It fitted into the rational conclusions of the educationists.

One series expressed such efforts to change the society in these terms:

1. We want a society in which everyone has abundant and good food, clothing, shelter, and means of transportation and communication . . . we have the resources, technology, and workers to provide for them all; . . . the difficulty lies in our social organization.

2. We want a society in which everyone has adequate, scientific health service and medical care, healthful working conditions, opportunities for healthful recreation, and healthful homes and communities.

3. We want a society in which everyone has socially useful work suited to his capacities and interests. . . . They realize that the profit system makes such a readjustment difficult, and they are able to conceive, without emotional disturbance, a world in which the profit motive would be inoperative.

6. We want a society in which there is no exploitation of human beings. . . . They have rejected the individualistic, competitive idea of success and despise it when they see it portrayed in books, magazines and movies.

8. We want a society in which there is no war. Our pupils therefore, have never learned in school to regard any war as justifiable, profitable, romantic, heroic, patriotic or necessary. They believe that those who took part in the last war were deluded victims of circumstance who wasted their lives to no purpose. . . . They will not take part in the next war, and they will not go to jail on that account if they can help it.[6]

The author of this article lists twelve such points to describe how pupils should be trained to change our society so as to eliminate not only war, but competition and the profit motive. Many similar statements of the vision of a changed society could be quoted from education journals (*Progressive Education, The Social Frontier, Frontiers of Democracy*) and from scores of books, but the essence of this aspect of the vision can be gleaned from a few pronouncements by a leader of the movement, Professor G. S. Counts. In *Dare the School Build a New Social Order?* the vision of the changed society is expressed as:

> . . . a new age where ignorance must be replaced by knowledge, competition by cooperation, trust in Providence by careful planning, and private capitalism by some form of socialized economy. *(P. 48)*

> That the teachers should deliberately reach for power and then make the most of their conquest is my firm conviction. To the extent that they are permitted to fashion the curriculum and procedures of the school they will definitely and positively influence the social attitudes, ideals, and behavior of the coming generation. . . . *(Pp. 28-9)*

> . . . transform or destroy all conventions, institutions, and special groups inimical to the underlying principles of democracy; and finally be prepared as a last resort, in either the defense or the realization of this purpose, to follow the method of revolution. . . . *(P. 42)*

Obsessed by a vision of what they believed to be a rational, peaceful, cooperative society in which everyone would have an abundance of food, clothing, recreation and medical care, a highly influential group of educators seriously modified the vision of education as a process whereby children would learn to "think for themselves", to include indoctrination with a set of ideas which, whatever their merits, were widely at variance with earlier beliefs. That a definite element of idealism motivated the group should be readily granted; but it should also be recognized that when they used idealistic phrases such as "cooperation", "social planning", "democracy", and "production for use, not for profit", their eyes were on the stars. The brightest star of all was what they then called "the socialist experiment in Russia".

So imbued were some educational leaders with their vision of indoctrinating pupils so as to lead them, through thought-controlled paths, to Utopia that even the leader of the Socialist Party, Norman Thomas, chided them on their excesses and reminded them that schools are supposed to present both sides of controversial issues.[7]

Harold Laski, an ardent apologist of Soviet Russia and a leading interpreter of the strategy of British socialism, described the recommendations of another educational organization, the American Historical Association's Commission on Social Studies, as

> At bottom, and stripped of its carefully neutral phrases, the report is an educational program for a socialist America.[8]

Professor Counts, among others, came to denounce the practices of Soviet Communism. Among educationists (those highly influential professors at teachers colleges who teach teachers), attempts to make real their vision of a socialistic-tinted Utopia are fewer now, and less blatant. Efforts to "change the world" are more subtle—and perhaps thereby more effective. Teachers particularly will profit from the documented summary of the development and techniques of this aspect of the educational vision which is found in *The Turning of the Tides*.[5]

On the surface, however, this facet of the vision is no longer so prominent, and the most pronounced elements in the vision as it now relates to education were sympathetically summarized in *The New York Times* (April 6, 1953) by the educational reporter, Benjamin Fine. Now called the "modern teaching method", and more common in large cities than elsewhere, the process is once again designed to emancipate the personality and to encourage creativity. Classrooms are characterized by a "permissive" atmosphere rather than by one of formality. Rigid discipline has all but disappeared and children walk around at will, talking freely. Mr. Fine contends that there is a definite plan behind all the confusion which strikes the eye on entering a modern schoolroom, a plan which stresses self-discipline with the "authoritarian teacher-knows-best attitude" replaced by a democratic spirit of "let's-all-work-together."

Mass promotions are the rule where the modern method is practiced. Regardless of ability, regardless of work they have done or work they have neglected to do, regardless of subjects which they have passed or subjects which they have failed to pass, regardless of attendance or absence, interest or disinterest, how they behaved or misbehaved, virtually all pupils are promoted. When complaints are made that pupils enter high school with no knowledge of mathematics, with a sublime ignorance of grammar, sometimes unable to write legibly, and often incapable of reading understandingly, mass promotions are explained as part of the vision for developing the personality by asserting that "children not promoted get a failure complex."

For similar reasons, and especially to discourage competition, report cards contain no more than relatively meaningless symbols, such as S (satisfactory), U (unsatisfactory), and I (needs improvement). But do not be disturbed that these moderate indications of competition—an aspect of life so thrilling and helpfully stimulating to most children—actually are competitively earned. The few marks which remain on report cards are obtained by a new and non-competitive approach which is supposed "to measure the child against his own ability, not against the ability of his classmates." In this approach, should the ability be meager, his meager efforts will find reward with a grade of S. Some wonder might arise as to the justice of this measurement when a diligent and able pupil does work far superior to that done by a lackadaisical dullard but receives no greater award, or in some situations where exceptional diligence raises the teacher's estimate of ability to an artificial height, whereupon a good performance by the diligent one is awarded a U—while the reward of a sufficiently well-established record of lackadaisical sloth is a continuous succession of Ss.

The light of the vision fails to shine on diligence, for that might be a mark of character. Its benign glow is reserved for the illumination of personality.

"More emphasis is placed upon 'experience' in the teaching method. Children are taken to the zoo, to museums, to points of interest in the city and to neighborhood projects." Such experience is supposed to serve as "a point of departure" for learning reading, writing and arithmetic. Mr. Fine's article does not explain how visits to the zoo aid in learning to read, write or add, but I suppose it is possible that one of the children might someday become a keeper at a zoo or a curator at a museum, or a guide on a sightseeing bus, so perhaps the trips have some merit. It is also a bit difficult to determine the purpose of a project where children of a New York City school devoted six weeks to "How We Live in Hot Lands", but Mr. Fine reports that by observing the 9-year-old chairman of the project he learned that the school taught one to relax, so such endeavors must also be of value.

"Intangible gains—a greater degree of self-reliance, of confidence, of poise and of personal and social development can be found in the young children of today." Thus Mr. Fine sums up the benefits of the modern teaching method which emerges from the vision of education as a process designed to develop the personality. Unfortunately, such things as confidence, poise, and personal and social development *are* intangibles and whether they are found in greater degree among the products of the modern teaching method than among others, we do not know. Even if it were established that they are, we could not determine whether they arose from the method or from other conditions which affect the lives of our children. Nor could we determine whether they are associated with other characteristics—greater criminality, more violations of the codes of sexual conduct, more dope addiction, and greater likelihood of divorce—which also are found in greater degree among the products of the modern teaching method.

Many sincere people are inspired by the vision as it applies to education—to the ideal of changing the society, to the hope that with competition, report cards, discipline, drill and failure eliminated, a permissive educational atmosphere will produce a high degree of creativity, spontaneous expression and cooperation which pupils will carry over into their adult lives. Children, it is hoped, will learn to think for themselves, to be tolerant and democratic, and to adjust to modern real-life situations in a rational manner.

In the warm atmosphere of this sheltered environment the tender shoots of infancy, unhampered by adverse drought of failure, unbent by chilling winds of competition, unmarred by scars from the rigid restraint of discipline, will bloom into full-flowering personalities, unimpeded by roots of tradition.

Religion and The Vision

It is proper that religious groups should attempt to change the world, but it is paradoxical that some of the clergy should find the secular vision—the bright promise of solution through the rational mind—so fascinating that they seem to be blinded to the influence of history, tradition, and even morality and supernatural spirituality.

> Awed by the formidable character of modern culture in its various forms, especially by the glittering achievements and the messianic hopes of science, and by the development of secular education, liberal Protestantism sensed acutely the relevance of all this to Christianity.

Thus, in *Can Protestantism Win America?* (p. 88), C. C. Morrison describes the influence of the vision of successful secular science on some sections of religion. As in other areas, the principal facets of the vision are economic determinism, peace, and a psychoanalytic interpretation of individual human behavior.

Illustrative of the weighty influence of economic determinism, 23 of the 98 bishops of the Church of England, 14 of the deans, and some 200 other members of the clergy adopted and endorsed a secular program at the Malvern Conference in 1941. Among the proposals was stressed the uniting of Europe into a cooperative commonwealth; communal ownership of the means of production; condemnation of the profit motive (production for use and not for profit). These proposals were interspersed among others which are quite proper for the Church, such as the admonition to pastors that they direct their efforts against bad housing and malnutrition.

[40]

A year later, a commission of 80 official representatives of a variety of Protestant denominations in England sponsored a program even more definite in its reliance on economic determinism. Included in the program were such things as guaranteed wages, price ceilings, assurances of congenial work, scientific monetary control, and extensive governmental planning to control economic processes.

These programs (and similar church-sponsored programs in America), together with the manner in which they are worded and their reliance upon economic planning as a panacea for both personal and social problems, indicate that important sections of the clergy follow almost exactly the pattern of progressive educators.

It is a pattern which includes denunciation of capitalism and of private enterprise; which attributes in cavalier fashion much of the evil of society to the economic system; which involves the vision of changing the world through a "scientific" secular panacea—i.e., through governmental control. In addition to those mentioned above, essentially the same pattern constitutes the program endorsed by many other religious organizations, such as Christian Action, the Council for Social Action (Congregationalists) and the Methodist Federation for Social Action.

At what would seem to be an opposite pole of behavior, but actually constituting an integral part of the same vision and arising out of similar sources, clergymen increasingly turn to psychology, psychiatry, and especially to psychoanalysis for formulas to apply to personal problems and to marital difficulties.

Though surveys taken by the polling technique are far from precise in their findings, some indication of this increasing reliance upon the secular approach is found in a survey made by Elmo Roper. Presented as representative of the United States, the survey reported that

> On almost every question, clergymen of all faiths strongly supported the generally accepted psychiatric viewpoints.[9]

Teachers followed the same pattern, and both groups were

> almost unanimous in rejecting punitive treatment when confronted with the problem of juvenile delinquency.

Other indications of the acceptance of the psychoanalytic interpretation are found in journals such as *Pastoral Psychology*, "a religiously oriented periodical of the science of human behavior", and advertised as being of immediate value and appliction for clergymen's use in dealing with such problems as personality disturbances, marriage and divorce, parent-child relationships, alcoholism, sexual disturbances, crime and juvenile de-

[41]

linquency. Of similar import are articles from *The Pastor*. Psychological clinics operate in direct conjunction with some churches. This aspect of the vision—that the cure to personal troubles of practically all kinds is to be found in psychoanalytic interpretation—is most forcefully expressed by the late Rabbi J. L. Liebman in his best-selling book, *Peace of Mind:*

> I am convinced . . . that religion, which already has made its peace with Copernicus and Darwin, will have to make peace with Freud. *(P. 20)*

> Such a religion will be able not merely to describe the good life and its great goals but also to implement that life with indispensible means. Aided by the tools of dynamic psychology [psychoanalysis], . . . this wiser religion will be able to show men and women how to achieve a free conscience, a less counterfeit love, a more integrated courage, and an undistorted life-affirming communion with God. *(Pp. 21-2)*

A vision of people emancipated from fear of poverty by governmental control of economic processes, and freed of anxieties, doubts and all sense of guilt, through psychoanalytic guidance, dazzles at least some clergymen, surmounting barriers of sectarian differences to bind them with a sense of common mission.

Marriage and The Vision

Beliefs and values which bound together traditional families into lifelong unions are gradually being dissipated by the vision of individualistic marriages. No longer is it considered a social and religious obligation to marry and, once married, to bear and rear children. Personal preference—to marry or not, to have children or not—becomes almost the sole determining factor.

Families formerly exerted considerable influence in the choice of a spouse, guiding if not directing their children to choose from a restricted group of persons made eligible by similar economic and social status. Traits sought in a prospective spouse were simple: The wife to be faithful, a good manager, not frivolous or extravagant. Sobriety, industriousness, thrift, and restraint from willful cruelty were traits deemed desirable in prospective husbands. With similar backgrounds, and lacking vices, it was assumed that love would grow as happiness was earned through mutual sacrifice and hardship, lightened by mutual sharing.

Wishes of the individuals now outweigh if they do not eliminate family advice in the choice of a spouse. As ever, females have a weather-eye fixed on prospects of economic security in their choice, while the gleam aroused by sexual attractiveness still distorts the male's clear perception of other qualities. Increasingly, however, both partners set qualities of companionship and mutual interests as their ideal. They desire a marriage partner who will have the same or similar interests; not a respected husband to be helped, obeyed and listened to with admiration; not a wife to obey as a respectful helpmeet—but a pal. Such qualities must be present or, more realistically, must be believed to be present, before marriage can be considered.

Success or failure of marital relationships is judged in terms of the adjustment of two personalities—a completely individualistic and secular yardstick. If the personalities fail to adjust, if they seem to be incompatible, it is not only acceptable but desirable that the marriage be terminated by divorce. Within recent years some prominent authorities have developed this line of "rationality" to the point where they contend that high rates of divorce, far from being a symptom that the domestic institution is somewhat disorganized, demonstrate that family life in America is being reorganized around new and better values. Perhaps extensive divorce does somehow prove that the family is being reorganized rather than disorganized, but there is precious little proof for this contention.

Patriarchal family relationships in which a superior authority of the husband was recognized by law, by society, and by wife and children rapidly give way to the ideal of equal authority. This part of the vision is sometimes called the equalitarian family, while students often refer to it in their statements about the ideal family as a 50-50 arrangement. Most preferred, however, among those entranced by a vision of changing familial relationships is the proud and appealing designation, *the democratic family*. Wives, and children too, will share equally in decisions with the husband and father.

One husband attributed thirty years of successful married life to the fact that in the very beginning he and his wife agreed that he would decide all of the big problems while she would decide all of the little ones. He stated that no serious quarrels ever arose because, in the entire thirty years, no big problems ever came up! In some modern instances one is indeed led to wonder if the patriarchal family which the husband dominated is not giving way to a matriarchal family arrangement, dominated by the wife under designations of "equality" and "democracy". As wives are emancipated from the domination of husbands they are also being emancipated from their role as mothers and household managers. Over 10,000,000 women "pursue a career" even though married, and the number of childless marriages increases apace.

At an even more rapid rate than men, women are being emancipated from the rigid standards of conduct which governed them in the past. Gradually the distinction between male and female moral standards becomes less clear. Though male standards decline, those of females decline at a rate which is relatively more rapid, thus approaching a single standard. It is a standard, furthermore, which is no longer looked upon as being absolute, but now is considered to be relative and individualistic. The relativistic and individualistic character of the standards find expression in such attitudes as: "I know it's wrong, but . . ."; "After all, it isn't as though we didn't intend to get married"; "Since we really love each other . . ."; "This way we'll learn if we are really suited to each other"; "Almost everyone does it, anyway"; "I know it's not wrong, because of the way I feel."

Naturally and inescapably, though many are loath to admit it, the courtesies and special considerations formerly accorded women due to their adherence to more demanding codes of conduct fade away as they accept the "privileges" of men. Many would deny that there is any direct relationship between the two, and some of those who admit it would contend that it is a small price to pay for female emancipation and women's rights.

Part of the pattern of emancipation is fostered by programs of sex education. Such education is promoted "to create a wholesome attitude toward sex"; "to raise sex above the gutter level"; "to prevent guilt complexes"; "to correct sex ignorance, superstitions and juvenile delinquency"; "to promote social adjustment"; "to remove the veils of secrecy from sex and bring it out into the open"; and to "promote marital adjustment".

Courses in marriage and family living are established in more and more high schools and colleges, with textbooks and popular books and magazine articles by the hundred bringing the light of "the new scientific knowledge" about marriage to millions who formerly embarked upon the rough seas of matrimony suffering from the delusion of "the romantic fallacy". Marital prediction tests are formulated and widely publicized so that young people can determine whether or not they are compatible before they become married. In numerous cities marriage clinics and counselling services have been established where matrimonial wounds can be salved and bound before they fester into ruptures. Serious disputes are now brought to the attention of special family courts where experts attempt to prevent dissolution of the union.

Thus is the vision of secular marriage reenforced by a plethora of experts and agencies.

Criminality and The Vision

Should parents, though aided by the wealth of "scientific advice" and by an educational process carefully geared to prevent the development of feelings of insecurity and inhibitions, fail to make their children law-abiding members of the society, an entire battalion of other agencies and experts now exists to remedy the unlikely lapse.

In Chicago, in 1899, young criminals for the first time were dealt with by a special court. A first step in implementing the vision of reformation of criminals was to change the title by which they were addressed. Now one of the favorite methods of solving our problems is to designate the problem itself by a less unpleasant name. Young criminals have been redesignated as *juvenile delinquents,* and an entire technique has been established to deal with them.

Juvenile courts quickly spread across the Nation and, though they differ in the details of their administration, they generally function in conformity with principles similar to those of the early Chicago Juvenile Court. Such courts do not treat violations of the criminal codes by young people (up to 18 years of age*) as criminal acts, with guilt or innocence to be publicly determined by a jury according to established rules of evidence. Juvenile courts operate under the doctrine of *parens patriae,* meaning that the court acts as a parent should, to guide and help rather than to punish. No longer do such courts act as agencies established by the society, paid for by the society, and existing for the protection of the society from criminal activity. They now function to try to understand, to guide, and to protect young persons brought before them charged with criminal offenses. To protect young offenders from embarrassment, the public is now barred from the hearings, a measure which, while undoubtedly humanitarian, is chillingly reminiscent of star-chamber proceedings which Anglo-Saxons fought for centuries to remedy by instituting trial-by-jury.

Rules governing the presentation and admissability of legal evidence are abandoned, and the hearing is informal. The interests of the public are no longer protected by a prosecuting attorney. Probation officers make social investigations of the background of the offender and, together with psychiatrists and social workers, protect the interests of the offender. While awaiting a hearing the young offender is usually allowed to remain in the custody of his parents instead of being remanded to jail. If the offender is taken into custody to await trial, he goes not to jail but to a "Youth Study Center". In the vast majority of cases no hearing at all is held, even though good evidence is available that a criminal act has been committed. If a hearing is held it is almost certain that there will be no penalty, though guilt is estab-

---

* The proposal is seriously made to raise to 21 years the age of accountancy for criminal acts.

lished. In the small percentage of cases in which offenders are placed in an institution, the period of the sentence is short, and the confinement is not in a prison but in a correctional institution. Punishment, in those rare instances where punishment is administered, is measured more in terms of the "needs" of the offender than in terms of the gravity of the offense.

Slum clearance projects, state-financed housing programs, recreational centers, boys' clubs, crime prevention associations, social workers, guidance counsellors, and other agencies and experts now operate to prevent youths from committing crimes and to reform them after the preventive methods have failed. Humanitarian motivations, which were the original source of the movement, are now fortified by the findings, or supposed findings, of expert criminologists and psychiatrists.

Such opinions now play an increasingly important role in the administration of criminal courts for adult offenders as well as in determining the manner in which the juvenile courts operate. Adult criminals now have the benefits of probation, parole, and indeterminate sentences to hasten their reform. Probation allows some offenders, though guilty, to avoid serving a prison sentence. Indeterminate sentences establish a theoretical maximum and a theoretical minimum period to be served, rather than fixing a specific sentence. Indeterminate sentences are based on the ideal that a convict should not be compelled to serve a fixed number of years if his behavior indicates that he has reformed. In practice, only a negligible percentage of convicts, no matter what their records or their behavior, ever serve the maximum period for which they are sentenced. It may be surprising to know that probably only a minority even serve their minimum sentence. "Time off for good behavior" is subtracted from the minimum, not from the maximum, so that many if not most convicts are released at the expiration of approximately two-thirds of their *minimum* sentence. "Good behavior" in actuality means the absence of bad behavior, rather than being an indication that criminal tendencies have been eliminated.

Thus in the educational process, in religious endeavors, in marriage and family relationships, in the treatment of criminals and in other areas, the institutions associated with individual behavior become dominated by a vision of secular adjustment, independent of spiritual restraints and divorced from traditional beliefs.

Creation of Rights

The National Resources Planning Board proclaimed the following "rights" in 1943:

1. The right to work, usefully and creatively, through the

productive years.

2. The right to fair pay, adequate to command the necessities and amenities of life in exchange for work, ideas, thrift, and other socially valuable service.

3. The right to adequate food, clothing, shelter, and medical care.

4. The right to security, with freedom from fear of old age, want, dependency, sickness, unemployment, and accident.

5. The right to live in a system of free enterprise, free from compulsory labor, irresponsible private power, arbitrary public authority, and unregulated monopolies.

6. The right to come and go, to speak or to be silent, free from spyings of secret political police.

7. The right to equality before the law, with equal access to justice in fact.

8. The right to education, for work, for citizenship, and for personal growth and happiness; and

9. The right to rest, recreation, and adventure, the opportunity to enjoy life and take part in an advancing civilization.

Similarly, in a message to Congress in 1944, President Franklin D. Roosevelt endowed Americans with

The right to a useful and remunerative job in the industries or shops or farms or mines of the nation;

The right to earn enough to provide adequate food and clothing and recreation;

The right of every farmer to raise and sell his products at a return which will give him and his family a decent living;

The right of every business man, large and small, to trade in an atmosphere of freedom from unfair competition and domination by monopolies at home or abroad;

The right of every family to a decent home;

The right to adequate medical care and the opportunity to achieve and enjoy good health;

The right to adequate protection from the economic fears of old age, sickness, accident, and unemployment;

The right to a good education.

Echoing in expression the spirit of the times, the United Nations established a Commission on Human Rights which in 1951 generously granted an impressive variety of economic and social rights to everybody in the world:

The right to work at a job freely chosen, the right to reasonable conditions of work and equal pay for equal work as well as reasonable hours of labor, the right to social security, the right to adequate housing, the right to an adequate standard of living, the right to the "best state of health a person is capable of attaining", the right of mothers and children to special protection, the right to join trade unions, the right to free elementary education and to extension for free secondary education.

Indicative of the general antipathy toward private enterprise which influences those entranced by the vision, a proposal to include the right to own property was defeated on the ground that it was not a fundamental human right on a par with those mentioned above.

Each child born in New York State now receives a copy of a "Children's Bill of Rights" which affirms the child's right to all aspects of welfare, security and affection without regard to race or creed. Psychoanalysists, marriage counsellors and social workers now bestow indiscriminately upon people the "right" to be loved; the "right" to be well-born; the "right" of every child to be wanted; the "right" to good health and a variety of other "rights".

Besides expressing itself in such areas, the vision is supplemented by newly established "rights" and is in a process of codifying itself into an ethical pattern which I have designated as "The New Morality".

The New Morality

A new type of moral code which appears to be replacing earlier beliefs and codes emerges from the vision of changing that part of the world which affects personal behavior. To conform to the new morality, to be "good" according to its tenets, you must applaud all attempts to emancipate the personality from restraints imposed upon it by adherence to earlier moral codes and you must praise every attempt to free behavior from traditional rules of proper conduct which (being "the oppressive weight of the dead hand of the past") restrict personal expression.

Those who continue to stress the importance of character and of strict codes of behavior, of discipline and drill, of competition; those who call attention to the hazards involved in the present course of events, are "bad". Those who express their apprehension or who offer evidence that self-expression and creativity may be disguises for selfishness and sloth; that competition is necessary training for life, and stimulating rather than frustrating to most children; that principles are more important than transient factual knowledge; that sexual freedom speedily degenerates into sexual license, are castigated by those who encompass the heady vision of the new morality. Critics and dissenters are labeled "enemies of education", "foes of progress", "prudes", "fundamentalists", "mid-Victorians" or "reactionaries".

In addition to emancipation of the personality and removal of most restraints upon sexual behavior, the new morality upholds tolerance as an important aspect of virtue. Tolerance for violators of sexual codes; tolerance for criminals; and especially tolerance for any shortcomings or defects possessed by particular minority groups in the society, becomes a criterion of propriety if not of "goodness".

Virtue also attaches to those who advocate the elimination of slums, to those who espouse a "living wage", to those who promote equal rights for women, and to those who proclaim internationalist sentiments. Patriotism, according to the new code, is unfashionable if not unethical, and is disparaged by labels such as "isolationism", "chauvinism" and "ethnocentricism".

The Vision of Emancipation

This is the vision of personal emancipation. It is a vision which seeks to release behavior from fetters which restrict development of the personality; to release individual expression from the hampering influence of outmoded beliefs of the past, from the artificial restraints of religious creed and spiritual dogma.

Personalities of children, released from the tight restraining bands of discipline and unwarped by indoctrination, will bloom into full flower. Knowing that all misbehavior can be explained in terms of unfortunate experiences during early childhood, that evil and sin are relics of superstitious supernaturalism, that bad and good are merely matters of relative interpretation, people are freed from all deep sense of guilt and from any of the oppressive weight of responsibility. Personalities of females, freed from artificial restrictions and outmoded conventions which curtailed their development and limited the areas in which they could express themselves, will flower as fully as those of men.

Emancipation of our mental outlook from limitations imposed by the confines of national boundaries will enable us to develop broader, richer, internationalistic perspectives.

This intoxicating vision of emancipation from the restrictive influences which bound and warped our thinking and stifled our expression, this release from convention which will enable us to face modern problems from a rationalistic approach, is the focus of the view of the future for many sincere and humanitarian people. Small wonder; so large is their hope for humanity, so grandiose their plans for mankind's future, that they look with scorn upon those who seem blind to the promise of the vision. Skeptics and critics, the visionaries are convinced, must be motivated by some narrow prejudice inherited from an earlier day. Those unenlightened by the vision falter and grope in false paths and quiver in startled fear at imagined, murky hazards.

For those endowed with the vision, its light illumines the one true path along which they skip lightly over obstacles and daringly cut corners as they call for others to leave the shadows and to follow their lead into the future.

Chapter III

The Source: Scientism and Hope

FROM what source does the vision of emancipation arise?

Why, in these days, does it entrance so many influential persons and so greatly affect our personal behavior, educational practices, even our religious outlook?

Does this vision emerge clearly to those who combine sensitivity with intelligence, and humanitarian sentiment with respect for rational evidence? Is it obscured from those who combine callousness with ignorance, narrow selfishness with emotional prejudice?

Does allegiance to tradition and adherence to spiritual doctrine cause cataracts to form over the eyes to conceal the vision from sight, to view the world through a fog of misconceptions which can be swept away by the clearing winds of reason? Above all, does the vision appear as a true reflection of reality, or is it a mirage arising out of mists of fantasy?

Though the vision can be portrayed in general outline, no clear-cut blueprint can be found to diagram the precise location of its source. A number of conditions, rather than any one simple factor, seem to be associated with its emergence. Some of these conditions will be described in brief fashion, but our principal focus will be upon an element of the source which appears to be of particular significance. This element, and the manner in which it has affected our attitudes toward behavior, will be described in some detail.

Let us first mention some changes in our way of life which make us particularly susceptible to the vision of emancipation from traditional and spiritual ties.

From Person to Personality

Today we are, most of us, enmeshed in circumstances which make the conditions of our lives quite different from those of earlier days. Among older people there is a temptation to exaggerate the simplicity of earlier conditions; to allow nostalgia for their youth to limn with bold strokes the giants that men were; to etch with deft touch the fragile gentility and resolute compassion of women; to blend these oak-staunch men and rose-petalled women into a warmly glowing portrayal of heartfelt happiness, framed in earthbound simplicity.

Our sympathy for sentiments which evoke such contrasts between an idyllic past and a hopelessly depraved present should not tempt us to forget that the past itself was far from perfect; nor, on the other hand, should the arrogance of modernity lead us to proclaim all change as progress, simply because it is change.

Many changes have taken place in America. Some of these; technological inventions such as automobiles, radios, television and electric lights, affect our lives directly. Others, such as machines to study the nuclear structure of atoms, affect our lives but indirectly. Associated in general with the development of a variety of machines, but not caused by any one of them, many of us now live quite different lives than did people in the past.

Much more commonly in earlier times than now, people lived in rural areas or in small towns. Many were born, spent their entire lives and died, in the same village. Even those who moved from one place to another usually found conditions very similar. Frequently everyone knew everyone else; knew their family background, had a fairly good estimate of their age, who they were "sweet on", what their approximate income was, and knew about many other aspects of their lives. Violations of codes of conduct were difficult to conceal, and more important than official punishment was the scorn or ostracism of one's neighbors.

Character, in that way of life, was much more important than was personality. Attempts to put on a "big front", to pretend to be more important than you actually were, resulted in no reward but ridicule. Not only the person but his family background, sometimes unfairly perhaps, was part of an assessment of his worth by his neighbors. People, especially those on farms, lived close to the realities of nature, the facts of life and death. Formal education was rare, and schoolteachers and clergymen derived respect by virtue of their "book-learning".

Most people now live in cities, and the amount of internal migration is very great. With little concern, we travel or move from one section of the country to another. Many things; automobile trips, baseball games, radio, movies and television, divert us from our concern with other people as persons. Especially in large cities we know only pieces of the personality (and frequently nothing of the character) of the people with whom we associate. We have many acquaintances, few friends. Some people we meet as we travel to work, others are known only as fellow-workers. Dentists know you by the number of your cavities, doctors by your floating kidney. The delicatessen proprietor thinks of you as "Mr. Salami and Rye". Few know you, or are interested in you, as a whole person. Life and behavior become segmented, and bits of personality become more important than character. Few know, and fewer care, of your past behavior. You are judged by your status at the present.

Even neighbors know little of each other, and scorn, contempt and ostracism lose their effectiveness as controls over behavior. In the unlikely event that misbehavior arouses hostility in one neighborhood it is easy to move to another, and begin anew. Since the response you arouse in other people depends so largely upon only the surface segments of your personality, you develop a variety of false fronts, a series of masks to be put on as needed, and thus you learn to practice duplicity.

Since the opinion of other people depends so heavily upon your status of the moment (and since the principal way to judge your status is measured by how much you spend, the horsepower of your car, or the size of your television set), material possessions loom ever higher on your scale of values. Psychic pressures tempt you to spend your money in ways which will impress other people, ostentatiously; on jewelry, clothes, automobiles, and other symbols of material success. Appearance becomes more important than substance.

Beneath all such pretence lies a gnawing awareness of superficiality and lack of permanence in the way of life and a longing for some formula, some panacea which will give the present a sense of fullness and provide a guarantee for the future.

Such conditions, so common to modern life, do not, however, seem to be the source of the vision. While they pave the way for its acceptance, they do not create it. The spiritual vacuum associated with life in large cities could have been filled by a variety of things, so an investigation of the source resolves itself into an examination of the particular kinds of ideas which prevail, and into reasons for their popularity. For the source of the vision lies closer to ideas than to particular material circumstances. Such ideas do not arise from separate origins. They have a common source and in their operation they interweave with each other to form a pattern of ideas—an ideology. The roots of this ideology trace back to a particular set of interpretations concerning science—in a word, to scientism.

Before describing some characteristics of scientism, a brief discourse on science and scientific method is needed.

Science—Simple Method, Complex Influence

Since the dawn of intelligence man has wondered whence the sun rose in the morning and where it went at night; where the stars hid during the daytime; what changed a laughing child to a cold and lifeless lump of flesh; why birds could fly, while he could not. Men speculated upon such things and arrived at almost as many different answers as the number who pondered the questions. Thousands of years ago, specialists in the form of trained philosophers attempted to organize thinking about problems into logical systems, but reduced only slightly the diversity of their solutions. A few centuries ago, however, a new method of studying problems evolved—a method which for the first time enabled all who investigated a given problem to agree upon the answer. This was the method of science.

Many definitions of science can be found in books written about this subject. Numerous analyses describe scientific method and scientific techniques for specialists, and the brief description which follows is designed only to outline to laymen some of the essential elements of scientific investigation. A keen awareness of these essential elements of science is particularly important today when the results of scientific studies—or the results of what *seem to be* scientific studies—are applied to child-training, to education, to the treatment of juvenile delinquents and adult criminals, to sexual behavior and marital relations, and to a host of other aspects of both our personal lives and our Country's affairs.

For our purposes, science can be described as a useful method to study problems and to arrive at conclusions about them. It is a good method, but it is not the only method.

Several hundred years ago scholars began to apply the scientific method in a systematic way to fields such as astronomy, physics and chemistry. Discoveries arrived at through the scientific method were then used as a basis for multitudes of truly marvelous technological inventions which have transformed our living habits and brought us comfort and wealth far beyond any which was imagined in the wildest dreams of the philosophers.

Fascinated by the spectacular success associated with the application of the scientific method to the behavior of physical objects, and appalled by continued unhappiness in our personal lives and by the confusion and conflict in our social relations, many scholars attempted to apply the same method, or (and I stress this again) what *seems to be* the same method, to human behavior and social events. Perhaps some day this can be done, and perhaps on that bright day our personal behavior and social relations will be improved as spectacularly as television and radar improved upon smoke-signals. So beautiful is this dream that many persons are charmed into a belief that the hope for the future is the reality of the present. With the double-vision of the thoroughly inebriated they have lost sight of the actualities of human behavior and, even more importantly, their focus on the actualities of science has become wildly distorted. For though scientific method can be reduced to a few fairly simple steps, these steps must be measured with sure balance and unwavering stride.

Let us see whether this can be done with personal, and social, behavior.

Science was first applied, and it has attained its most notable successes, in fields such as physics. In such fields, researchers are able to use the technique of *controlled observation*. Controlled observation enables investigators to arrive at results upon which all competent students can agree. Results obtained through the employment of this technique must be agreed upon by all, no matter what their political beliefs, their social attitudes, or their religious convictions. It is a technique which eliminates all sentiment and bias.

In order to employ controlled observation, however, the objects being studied must first be reduced to units which are quantitative, divisible, and stable. Such quantitative, divisible and stable units include weight, distance, pressure and velocity. These can be translated into pounds, yards or meters, miles per hour or miles per second. Instruments such as scales, thermometers and gauges have been developed to measure with great accuracy the variations in such units of measure. Though some aspects of human behavior, such as the temperature of the body, blood pressure, height and weight, can be reduced to units similar to those employed in physical science, many others cannot.

Hopes and fears, sentiments and ideals, honor and bravery, love and hate, are qualitative rather than quantitative. They are neither uniform, divisible nor stable. You may be in love, or you may be brave, and you may believe that you are more in love or braver than someone else, but you can not say that you are exactly 86.4 percent in love or 93.7 percent brave. Such feelings lack the factor of stability essential to the scientific method. Unlike chemical compounds or electrons, they can increase or decrease—or even vanish—when investigators subject them to searching analysis and coldly attempt to reduce them to quantitative units.

Most of the vitally significant aspects of human behavior can not be reduced so as to enable those who study such behavior to use the technique of controlled observation. Even were this at present possible a second element is vital, and that involves *the formulation of an hypothesis.* An hypothesis is a clear statement of an assumption about the behavior of the things being studied, a statement formulated so that it can be clearly proved or disproved through the use of controlled observation. Statistical manipulation, or manipulation of facts, is not science. Researchers could take temperatures, count corpuscles, measure noses, and weigh people for the next thousand years without thereby contributing significantly to scientific knowledge. Without a specific hypothesis to be tested, to be developed into a theory if confirmed by the facts but to be rejected if at variance with them, involved statistical manipulation contributes to science little or nothing.

Verification is the ultimate criterion of scientific procedure. No matter how exact the observations, no matter how clever or reasonable the hypothesis, no matter how precise and intricate the statistical techniques, the final proof of the scientific pudding is verification. Scientific conclusions must be tested, retested, and tested again. Particularly where human welfare is involved, every effort must be made, and intense skepticism must be applied, to eliminate all possibility of error before such conclusions are recommended to the public. Prediction is a good test for verification, but even prediction can mislead. Correct predictions may be no more than coincidence, they may result from luck, they may occur because factors other than those being studied have influenced the result. Scientific predictions must not only be correct, they must be uniformly correct; and they must be correct, and demonstrably so, for the reasons specified in the hypothesis.

Anyone can "predict" that the sun will rise in the morning and set in the evening, that it will be colder in winter than in summer, that children will get into mischief, that some husbands will believe their wives misunderstand them, and that most people will get up before breakfast. Scientific predictions, however, must be based on explicitly stated theory; they must be not only generally correct but uniformly accurate, and the scientist must demonstrate that his predictions result from the reasons given in his hypothesis and from nothing else.

Such are some of the elements of scientific procedure. They are not mystical, they contain no magic ingredients, but they are fundamental, and they are vitally essential. Principles such as these must be adhered to with fanatic zeal. Those who modify them, who temporize, who employ shortcuts, or who use some of the principles but ignore other required tests, forsake the rare privilege of applying the word "science" to the title of their findings.

Few if any conclusions which can be applied to socially significant aspects of human behavior have been reached through this scientific process. Yet hundreds of books and articles each year claim to describe scientific conclusions about everything from toilet-training to war, and many people believe that scientific solutions can be safely applied to cure our personal concerns and our national problems.

Most such conclusions are not truly scientific, though they are called such. Most of them have merely a surface appearance of being scientific. They are illustrations not of science, but of *scientism.*

Scientism is the Source

Philosophers in earlier days had a limited audience, and their theories were read only by a few. These few could accept or reject them on the basis of their own personal logic, wisdom, or experience. Differences of great importance mark the current scene. For every book published a century ago there now are hundreds; for every high-school graduate then there are now a thousand; and in contrast to the few who once read or heard about scientific theories such matters are now publicized to millions. Meanwhile, technological developments have raised the prestige of science to such heights that we are awe-struck as, almost reverently, we look up to its huge achievements.

Theories which borrow the prestige of science profoundly affect our lives. This influence is so widespread that educated people now have a responsibility, to themselves as well as to their Country, to be wary of theories which seem to be scientific but which all too often omit one or more of the fundamental requirements of scientific procedure.

After several years of intensive study devoted to this problem I analyzed and illustrated this necessity in a book titled *Social Problems and Scientism.* In my analysis I tried to describe the confusion between science and scientism in considerable detail, but for our present purposes I wish to make only a brief statement of a few of the ways in which scientism disguises itself as science.

"Scientism" is a word which is sometimes used to describe a belief, and at other times it is employed to describe techniques which give non-scientific findings the appearance of being scientific. As a belief, it is described by Jacques Barzun (in *Darwin, Marx, Wagner*) as a conviction that

> ... nothing is outside the scope of science and that [science] can furnish answers to all human problems. It goes hand in hand with the Marxian denial of the efficacy of ideas, and it makes science a substitute for philosophy, art, and religion. *(P. 367)*

A belief of this sort, that science can replace not only philosophy, art, and religion, but also eliminate practical experience, wisdom, tradition and morality, is the source of the vision of emancipation for individuals and of the vision of Utopia for society.

As applied to methods which are used to support the conviction of scientistic (*not* scientific) visionaries, the term "scientism" includes a variety of techniques. Perhaps you have been taught, or possibly you have somewhere acquired a general idea that "science is knowledge", or that "science is accurate factual knowledge", or that "science is systematized knowledge", or that "science is knowledge organized and systematized around an hypothesis". Use of these and similar definitions is one of the techniques of scientism, one of the ways in which the visionaries bolster their conviction that science is the solution for the major problems of mankind, one of the ways in which new recruits are seduced into joining the ranks of the zealots of scientism. These I have described as "soft" definitions of science.

A proper definition of any term should not only include the distinctive characteristics of the subject, but it should exclude characteristics which apply to other things as well as to the subject. A classic illustration of failure to exclude characteristics common to other things was the ancient definition of man as "a two-legged animal without feathers". This particular definition was ridiculed out of existence when a humorist of antiquity plucked the feathers from a chicken and paraded it about the city.

All of us possess much knowledge, including much factual knowledge, which bears no relationship whatsoever to science. We know our name, our street address, how many brothers and sisters we have, our age, and many other things which are factual but not scientific. We may have developed tricks to help us to memorize the names of the States or other material which we are required to learn and thus could say we have systematized our factual knowledge around an hypothesis. We could describe our success in remembering such data as proof of the validity of the hypothesis, but few would seriously contend that such devices constitute science. A telephone book, street directory, almanac, dictionary, or even a personal record of possible "dates" with notations about their characteristics, would comply with definitions which describe science in terms of knowledge organized and systematized around an hypothesis. "Soft" definitions of science fail to include elements essential to scientific procedure and thus give advocates of scientism seeming substance to their vision. To those whose respect for scientific procedure is properly tempered with skepticism, such definitions are transparent. But to those entranced by the vision of changing the world, such definitions serve to cover poverty of thought with the resplendent "Emperor's Cloak" of science.

Coupled with "soft" definitions, frequent repetition of the magic word "science" is sufficient to convince many people that even absurd conclusions are correct. Together with such techniques it is now almost standard practice to use a variety of *prestige phrases,* such as "research", "probabilities", "statistics show . . .", "rational", "interdisciplinary", "workshops", "factual", "objective", "psychologists now agree", "social engineering", and "social planning".

To convince people that findings are supported by scientific studies, some advocates of scientism employ a *double standard* for their evidence. Evidence which is favorable to the viewpoint they wish to promote is strongly emphasized, contrary findings are either underemphasized or ignored. Since the present purpose is to describe the source of the vision of personal emancipation, let us observe the manner in which one of the most important aspects of this vision developed.

A Russian Dog Leads the Way

More than fifty years ago a Russian physiologist named Ivan Petrovitch Pavlov conducted an experiment with a dog. This experiment has influenced the training of thousands of infants in American families and millions of pupils in American schools. The statement seems farfetched, and so I hasten to add that intermediate influences were involved. But a real connection does exist between these seemingly unrelated happenings. In simplified form, the influence of this Russian dog on American life evolved in the following manner.

In Pavlov's experiment a dog was chained and was not fed until he became very hungry. Each time he was fed a bell was rung, and this pattern was followed throughout a series of feedings. After a time the dog came to associate the sound of the bell with food, and finally the sound of the bell alone produced a flow of saliva in the animal's mouth. On the basis of this type of experiment Pavlov developed the theory of the *conditioned reflex.* Ordinarily, the flow of saliva in a dog's mouth results from the sight or smell of food. The sight or smell of food is the *original stimulus* for which the flow of saliva is the reflex *response.* After repeated associations between the original stimulus (food) and a *substitute stimulus* (the sound of a bell), the reflex occurs in response to the substitute stimulus alone. The reflex is said to be "conditioned" to the substitute stimulus.

Several important questions still exist as to the scientific validity of the conditioned reflex theory, but for our purposes they need not be raised. You may wonder (and you should) how, even if scientifically validated, a theory which deals with a dog's drool has come to influence child training and educational practices. The next significant link in this connection was forged in the 1920s when an American psychologist, John B. Watson, published a book called *Behaviorism.*

In a simplified form which does not do justice to Watson's theory but which stresses its social influence, the theory was interpreted to mean that any human infant could be conditioned in a wide variety of ways. It was held that infants were capable of expressing only three emotions: Love, fear and rage. Furthermore, the only original stimulus which aroused the supposed emotion of love was physical fondling; rage was aroused only by physical restraint; and fear was aroused by noises or by a falling sensation. All things other than fondling, restraint, loud noises or a falling sensation give rise to emotional reactions only because we have been conditioned to respond to them in much the same manner that Pavlov's dog was conditioned to respond to the bell. Thus a dishpan banged behind the head of a child who is playing with a rabbit permanently conditions the child to be afraid of rabbits! As you walk through the woods you see a snake and a companion yells "Look out!" Perhaps he also grabs your arm and yanks you away or pushes you, thus adding a sensation of falling to the noise and doubly conditioning you to fear snakes.

Watson contended that any normal child could become brave or cowardly, honest or criminal, generous or selfish, a doctor or an Indian chief, if he were properly conditioned. Implied in the theory was the notion that proper conditioning would produce a perfect society of perfectly adjusted human beings. R. S. Woodworth, in his *Contemporary Schools of Psychology* tells how this theory, though resting only on sparse and questionable evidence, was hailed as "the most important book ever written" and how, for some, it became "a religion to take the place of religion".

Mothers began to raise their children on virtually a split-second schedule. Infants had to be fed and put to bed at precisely the same minute or otherwise, mothers were convinced, the children would not be properly conditioned. Thousands of mothers listened in anguish as their infants cried, for to pick up a crying baby and to fondle it would condition the child to cry whenever it wanted affection and love. Parents were seriously convinced—because it was "science", you see—that children could be conditioned to like spinach (which in those days had also been "scientifically proved" to be essential to child-health) if their associations with it were pleasant. For years parents smiled and yum-yummed over their own spinach to establish the proper association in the mind of the child—but for years their children continued to gag and splutter, and to prefer ice cream.

Though subsequent experiments failed to support the idea of conditioning, influential educators grasped it and continue to cherish it because it seems to provide them with a scientific lever to move the world. If educational processes became associated with pleasant experiences, they believed, children would be conditioned to enjoy them and learning would become a happy experience for all.

Pavlov provided the springboard for theories that general emotional responses could be conditioned, and interpreters took a running jump and leaped 'way up—into clouds of fancy. Conditioned reflexes required a long series of associations between the original and the substitute stimulus, and such conditioning faded away if it were not reenforced. But the doctrine soon assumed, without validated evidence, that a single experience would condition a child for his entire life.

Nor was this the final step in expanding the theory (which originally dealt with a minor phase of a dog's behavior) into a major influence in human loves and hates, preferences and prejudices.

The Kwakiutl Lead the Dog*

A number of cultural anthropologists began to exert their influence to expand the theory further. Their impressions and prejudices (in such books as Ruth Benedict's *Patterns of Culture*) were carefully phrased so as to lead readers to believe that their findings were scientific.

From these sources many were convinced that science had now proved that not only reflexes, not only emotions, but virtually all of our beliefs, sentiments, ideas and attitudes, were imposed upon us by culture. Through this further scientistic influence, visionaries became convinced that culture determines personality. If the culture is competitive, the personalities of people be-

---

* The Kwakiutl are a tribe of Indians on Vancouver Island, B.C., and are examples cited by Ruth Benedict in her *Patterns of Culture*.

come selfish and aggressive; if the culture is cooperative (that is, socialistic or collectivistic) people become considerate, helpful, moderate, and oh-so-free-from-care. Though the term "culture" itself has never been clearly defined, a belief grew that science had proved culture to be all-powerful; that it even determined practically all of the differences between men and women.

One effect of this theory of cultural determinism is to develop the view that people are puppets—that they are mere plastic and passive objects molded by cultural forces over which they have little awareness and no control. This theory, supported only by techniques of scientism, is spread by visionaries who thus rob people of their independence of thought, deprive them of their will, and strip from them their dignity.

Another effect is to lead people in the direction of *cultural relativism,* a point of view which holds that since different people engage in different practices none of these is either good or bad, moral or immoral. Thus moral relativism emerges.

Since some primitive groups practice wife-lending and others permit polygamy, neither adultery nor monogamy should be considered evil or good; they should be looked upon as relative to our culture. So the scientistic reasoning implies. Thus we become persuaded that our beliefs about good and bad exist because we have been conditioned to such beliefs. Nothing is either good or bad, but culture makes it so, and if the Kwakiutl do it, why can't you?

A gap remains in this gossamer web of reasoning. If we are all conditioned by culture, why aren't we exactly alike in our beliefs and behavior? This rent in the web is partially patched by assuming that different cultural influences operate within different class-groups and various sub-cultural groups. But is it not readily apparent that, no matter how much the groups are divided, individuals within them will differ, as within the same family one child may differ even as night from day, when contrasted with his brothers? Further, when cultures are broken down into too numerous sub-groups, the notion of an all-encompassing, all-powerful culture becomes fragmentized into nothingness.

Another thread therefore is needed to weave the web of scientism around the visionaries of personal emancipation.

Viennese Neurotics Lead the Kwakiutl Who Lead the Russian Dog

Let us leave the piteous yapping of the Russian dog, the plaintive cries of thousands of unattended babes. The noisy trail has finally led us to a place where we can relax—the psychoanalytic couch. Here, as we listen to the quiet, reassuring, calm explanation which ties together all the strands of personal behavior, we learn that persons are different because up is down, black is white, reality is unreal, and that bad is not only good but that it is sometimes better.

There are several variations of psychoanalytic interpretation, and each has contributed in some measure toward an increased understanding of human behavior; the practice of psychotherapy helps some people to recover from mental illness. It is not my purpose, however, to describe the theory in detail but to portray the general way in which it constitutes an important element within the source of the vision of personal emancipation.

Far more influential than other psychoanalytical interpretations are those developed by the Viennese, Sigmund Freud. In simplified form—which fails by far to do justice to the marvelous ingenuity of the theory but which may serve to illustrate how it relates to current beliefs—the interpretation supplies visionaries with a belief that certain desires determine the behavior of every person. These desires are supposed to be basic, universal, inescapable.

In the Freudian interpretation the desires are essentially sexual in nature. Every boy-child has, for example, the basic desire to kill his father and to mate with his mother. Girl-children, being gentler and more refined, wish to kill their mother and to mate with their father. Of course no one ever proved that such supposedly basic desires exist, and objective evidence, as I point out in *Social Problems and Scientism,* indicates that they have no greater degree of reality than the myths from which Freud derived such delightful notions. Yet such are the bases of this "scientific theory".

In America, and everywhere else for that matter, it isn't considered mannerly for little brother to slip real bullets into his pop-gun and mow daddy down. Nor is Sister Sue looked upon as a proper young miss if she flavors mama's tea with poison. The poor kids have to restrain their basic desires because our rules for conduct are so restrictive. Prevented from finding direct expression because social controls forbid the type of behavior which the mythical basic desires demand, the desires fester and swell in an equally mythical *unconscious mind.* Unless their toxins can be drained away, these boils on the unconscious mind become engorged till they burst, and their poison infects the entire personality in the form of a complex. Toxins in the unconscious mind, according to the theory, can be drained off by dreaming of what you want to do instead of actually doing it; by cutting up worms instead of mommy or daddy. All possible channels must be kept open for the drainage if complexes are to be avoided.

[63]

Child training and educational practices, therefore, must allow children opportunities to express themselves in any way that they desire (presumably short of mayhem). Above all, the child must not be frustrated by severe punishment or discipline.

Upon such notions never once supported by objective evidence; upon such myths dignified by the name of science, parents and teachers are persuaded by visionaries of emancipation to adopt *permissive* methods of child-care and training. Rather than conflicting with the equally scientific theory that we are passively molded by cultural forces, psychoanalytic interpretation supplements it by seeming to explain differences between personalities of people who are raised under the same cultural conditions.

In simplified and exaggerated form, the source of the vision of personal emancipation can thus be described as originating in theories of conditioned reflexes which were expanded into theories of conditioned emotional responses and into theories of cultural conditioning and cultural relativism. These then become interwoven with psychoanalytic interpretation. Implied in this type of interpretation are the notions that we are the puppets of forces about which we have scant knowledge and over which we have little control. Culture impinges upon us from the outside. Equally uncontrollable "basic desires" motivate us from within.

An interpretation of this type implies that we are helpless pawns, desperately in need of expert assistance—to formulate a desirable culture for us; that we are not responsible for our own behavior, and hence have no right to judge the misbehavior of others; that harsh punishment and firm discipline will thwart development of our children's personalities and may create complexes; that all behavior, no matter how monstrous, can be thus explained "scientifically", and once understood should be forgiven; that the principles of ethics and morality we believed in were merely a product of the way we were conditioned, that they are irrational and out of conformity with modern reality.

Many people are enamored of the theory because it seems to be scientific and because it is modern. Further, its supporters attain a glowing halo of tolerance, broad-mindedness, and deep understanding.

All but a few who embrace the vision have been blissfully ignorant of the way it can readily be fitted into a larger pattern, a pattern in which there are reflections of redirecting thoughts of people through "brainwashing"; a pattern of a society planned and carefully ordered by experts; a collectivistic or a socialistic society where everyone is adjusted—or dead. For, cheering the parade of Viennese neurotics, Kwakiutls, crying babes, and drooling dogs is the man whose theories of society are also disguised under the protecting cloak of science, Karl Marx.

Scientism is the source, or at least a significant aspect of the source, of the vision of personal emancipation now espoused through programs associated with progressive (now "modern") education, secularized religion, juvenile delinquency, sex education and other phenomena of the day. Many of their sponsors fail to appreciate that the weight of actual evidence is contrary to the tenets on which they base their programs; others somehow fail to realize that even were they scientific instead of scientistic, they would eliminate all intangibles such as love, patriotism and bravery from their calculations, and reduce people to puppets. Yet, by squinting only slightly, many are able to shut from their sight such deeper implications of the vision and to see only its shining surface which seems to reflect the bright promise of happier lives.

The very brilliance of this reflection has blinded them to the corruption, perversion, and rampant criminality associated with the stark reality which lies in the shadow of the vision of personal emancipation.

Chapter IV

The Reality: Life Without Rules

ON AN Autumn afternoon the sky's deep blue compels wonder to stir your soul, the tang of burning leaves assails your nostrils as you eagerly await the kickoff at the big football game. Through the clear air a whistle shrills as the referee waves his arm.

Fumble! The receiver drops the ball!

But—none of the other players falls on it!

The game, you see, is now played differently than it was before the visionaries of emancipation improved it in accordance with the "scientific" findings about human behavior. The new purpose of football is to develop personality.

The receiver who dropped the kickoff is a sensitive lad, so all the other players politely turn their backs and pretend that the fumble didn't happen. To do otherwise might make the receiver feel frustrated. Moreover, the fumbler is now allowed to run for a touchdown—to restore his injured pride. During the remainder of the game each player who lacks confidence is permitted by the others to make at least one touchdown, as is every man on the squad who has spent the proper amount of time attending practice. Two touchdowns are allowed players who say they had an unhappy childhood. Neither team wins, for to be defeated might give rise to feelings of inferiority among the losers. Both teams win.

Would such a game be any fun? What satisfaction would the spectators, or the players, get from it?

Would you enjoy baseball games where the pitcher who had seniority was automatically allowed to win; where fielders make no attempt to catch the ball if a batter really tries his best to get a hit; where each team is guaranteed a certain number of runs; where errors are applauded, to prevent injured feelings?

Yet not so very different from such a wonderland is the goal of the vision of personal emancipation. And so, before we proceed further along the path down which we already have rushed so far, it might be well to pause, to wrench our gaze from the glittering promise and look at the reality around us.

From its source in superficial theories about human behavior much of the doctrine has already flowed into our thinking—to dim our view of reality. And it is not the extremes which we need fear—not the children who spend three weeks in school playing that they are Bagandas, and then two weeks settling world issues as they re-enact the United Nations Assembly. Such extremes (though flowing directly from the source) are easy to detect and to eliminate with raucous laughter. It is not these burlesques of education which we need fear, but the more moderate, more subtle, expressions of the doctrine—failure to mete out merited punishment, the decline in discipline, the elimination of competition and drill, the mass promotions and similar practices which reflect the fear that frustrations will cause vital damages, and the hope that benefits will result from emancipated personalities.

Some results of such practices are direct, others are indirect. All are difficult to measure. In fairness to the visionaries who endorse and promote them it should be remembered that human behavior is so complex that it is impossible to determine which specific causes produce which precise effects. A persistent correspondence does exist, however, as attempts to emancipate the personality through educational practices are associated with declines in educational performance and increases in criminal and immoral behavior.

In defense of their program, educationists claim a superior reading ability of modern children as compared with children of a century ago. Such comparisons are questionable at best. Furthermore, studies in recent years indicate a substantial decline in reading ability, a drastic decline in spelling ability, and a calamitous collapse in the knowledge of grammar and punctuation.

An intelligent child in our society could learn reading, writing, and arithmetic with no formal education at all, or in spite of the worst methods of teaching, so the declining performance in these subjects is less important for society than are the attitudes engendered by the type of education which results from the vision. Surveys of employers show that although they are concerned because the high-school graduates whom they hire cannot accurately add, subtract, multiply or divide, they are dismayed by the *attitude toward work*. Encouraged by teachers addicted to "progressive" educational methods, pupils are plunged into jobs without ever having learned proper manners, with resentment against authority instead of respect for it, with slovenly habits instead of an appreciation for accuracy such as was formerly instilled by discipline and drill.

It is the attitude not only toward school, not limited to their jobs, but the attitude toward life in general which is of greatest social concern. It is an attitude of disrespect for authority and exaltation of self-opinion among our youth. Most incidents of vandalism by school children are withheld from publication, but sufficient accounts have been revealed to show that the three Rs are all too often interpreted to mean "Rowdyism, Riot and Revolt".

But let us pass from the schooling in vandalism which encourages pupils to express their personalities through setting fire to their classrooms, by vicious and calculated destruction of property, and by intimidation of teachers, to the graduate scholars—the criminals.

"Watchman, what of the night?" The old Town Crier is no more. Who now calls out our warning? We turn to the *Uniform Crime Reports* issued by the Federal Bureau of Investigation to learn how fares the Republic. The visionaries would have us believe that all goes well; the reality set forth should shock us all.

For 1954, some 2,267,250 major crimes are recorded, representing a five-percent increase over 1953 which, in turn, represented a six-percent increase over 1952 which, in turn, represented an eight-percent increase over 1951 which, in turn, represented a five-percent increase over 1950! Crime, since 1950, outstripped the increase in population by a ratio of four to one.

Strong-arm thugs (we learn from the *Report* for 1954) committed more than 67,000 robberies, while 93,500 people were stabbed, shot, cut, clubbed or beaten, and over 18,000 women were raped. More than half a million homes and businesses were burglarized, while thieves stole 216,000 automobiles, and over a million other thefts were reported. Far from being an exaggerated exposé, the *Reports* emphasize that the estimates are conservative—that criminality is more prevalent than even these findings show.

We have been told and told again by the visionaries that poverty is a principal cause of crime. Yet when we stop listening to their glib tongues, cease reading their smooth-flowing words and look at reality, we find little support for their claims.

In the year 1937 we were still deep within depressed economic conditions. Widespread unemployment prevailed throughout the Land, and it was in this year that a recession offset much of the improvement which took place after the slow climb from the bottom of the depression in 1933. By contrast, 1954 was a year of unprecedented prosperity. Wages were high and almost everyone who wanted to work, women as well as men, had a job. Yet when the 1954 year of unparalleled prosperity is compared with the 1937 year of serious economic deprivation we find that crime, instead of declining, had tremendously increased. Almost twice as many rapes were committed in 1954 as in 1937, and more than twice as many innocent citizens were slugged, stabbed, shot, or beaten by thugs. Burglaries and larcenies had increased at a rate far higher than can be accounted for by any increase in population.

In my earlier work on *Social Problems and Scientism* I show objective studies in some detail to refute contentions of the visionaries that crime is caused by poverty, by slums, by broken homes, by frustrating experiences of early childhood or by other conditions which can be remedied by their programs. Economic conditions have improved, and we have fewer slums. Yet, as the supposed "causes" of crime are reduced through expensive housing and other programs, the rate of crime goes up instead of down. We have established boys' clubs, playgrounds, recreation centers, counsellors. We operate expensive juvenile court systems staffed with thousands of social workers, probation officers and expert psychiatrists. We have separated youthful offenders from older ones and now house them in Youth Study Centers rather than in jails. Some of these Centers are more luxurious in their appointments than law-abiding citizens can afford. Parents at home and teachers at school have adopted methods and educational practices which will not frustrate the youngsters or injure their precious egos. We have done all, and more than, the visionaries requested. Our reward has been no decrease in criminal activity but a rising tide of lawlessness which pounds threateningly at the very foundations of the homes of honest citizens.

Rather than confirming the grandiose promises of the visionaries, actual studies refute them. The new forms of "prevention" and "treatment" are associated with greater criminality rather than with less.

Preventive methods certainly do not prevent, and it appears that they encourage ever more criminality. Reform procedures are associated with a higher percentage of return to criminal ways than any other techniques ever devised by man. As W. H. Sheldon points out in his *Varieties of Delinquent Youth,* young criminals are easily persuaded by psychiatric social workers that their behavior really was caused by experiences during early youth; and they then begin to mouth this psychoanalytic jargon to explain away their conduct. The social workers, hearing what they themselves have planted in the minds of youth, are thereupon convinced of the validity and the proof of the theory!

Sex offenders justify their behavior by pointing to the pseudo-scientific findings of the Kinsey Reports, and when the son of a prominent father is arrested for robbing women at knife-point he is quick to justify his behavior by saying: "I have a mental block."

The evidence daily confronts us that the vision of emancipation, instead of reducing crime actually encourages it. The following excerpt from a letter to *The New York Times* illustrates the point:

> I live in what was formerly New York's famous "dead end" neighborhood. One warm evening late in the past summer I was an interested eavesdropper, via my living room window, on a meeting between two gangs of teen-agers who were planning a gang fight for the following night. After all the details of the projected mayhem were ironed out one of the older boys (about 18 years of age) asked that both gangs provide volunteer 11-year-olds so that in the event of police interference the gangs could have on hand expendable members for any arrests. Then came the punch line. In the words of the gang leader—"All they gotta tell the social worker in court is that they hate their mothers and they'll be out in a coupla hours." *(Jan. 13, 1953)*

Policemen become discouraged from a proper performance of their duties because they are aware that youthful criminals are seldom brought to trial if arrested, seldom convicted if tried, and only in a negligible percentage of cases are committed to a penal institution though found guilty. In proportion to criminal acts, fewer arrests are made, indicating that the actual situation is even worse than the mounting arrest-rates show.

Orwell's Reversal

As the vision of personal emancipation is embodied in education by discarding discipline, drill, and competition, and in the judicial system by abandoning trial-by-jury and using preventive and reformative measures based on notions growing out of the studies of the Russian dog, Viennese neurotics, and the Kwakiutl, crime increases apace.

All of us have our pet beliefs and theories, and many of us will cling to them even after our experience shows them to be wrong. But these visionaries—the very ones who ridicule traditions and deride the beliefs of earlier days—are a clan apart in their adherence to the vision fostered by zealots of scientism. They simply refuse to accept the fact that their programs do not work.

When their promised results not only fail to materialize but become allied with serious aggravations of the very conditions which they are supposed to cure, the claim is made that the bad condition is really a good state of affairs after all! This is one of the techniques which I have described in *Social Problems and Scientism*, designating it "Orwell's Reversal".

George Orwell was an anarchist. Like many other intellectuals he was obsessed with a vision of the personal emancipation which he felt would exist within a collectivistic Utopia. Like others, he had a great admiration for Soviet communism, but unlike some he was not completely blinded by the vision and by what was then called "The Great Russian Experiment". While fighting in the civil war in Spain in the 1930s, Orwell had actual experience with its brutality, duplicity and cynicism. As a result of his disillusionment he wrote a wonderful satire of communism, *Animal Farm*, and his frighteningly revealing and prescient novel *Nineteen Eighty-Four*. Orwell described a world of 1984 wherein the techniques of thought-control and brainwashing implicit in the theories which support the vision, had brought the vision to full reality. By re-writing history and through the censorship of news, people came to believe that "War is Peace", and that "Freedom is Slavery".

We already are being led to accept these "Orwell's Reversals" in several areas of our lives. Criminality is one of these areas. Visionaries claimed that their methods of education and their procedure in dealing with people would prevent crime. Their procedures were incorporated into practice at great financial cost to the society. As the "scientific" methods were put into ever-wider practice, crime increased. For a long time the visionaries denied that the increase existed, ridiculing those who expressed concern over mounting lawlessness. Accounts which revealed large increases in crime were derided as "newspaper hysteria", and were attributed to fallacies in computation. Finally, however, the increases continued so long and rose to such proportions that even the visionaries were forced to admit their existence. But so obsessed are they with the conviction that their theories can not be wrong, so in love are they with the vision of emancipation, that when they finally did recognize the reality of increased crime they not only refused to accept it as a repudiation of their theory, they claim it as proof of its validity!

You claim one thing; the opposite happens. You then say that because things turned out opposite to the way you claimed, your case has been proved. It is in truth an ingenious device.

You may wonder how this neat trick can be accomplished. Many illustrations could be cited, but just a few will show how it operates in connection with criminality.

When W. H. Sheldon, whose studies indicated that the new methods were "feeding oil on the raging fires of delinquency", pointed this out to a psychiatrist who sponsored such theories the response was, in effect: "Perhaps it is desirable that children become delinquents. If they did not, they might become neurotics." The psychiatrist had no proof that the children would become neurotic, yet he cites a possibility, however absurd and unproved, to convince others that the failure of the program proves that it is successful. (If a bank cashier absconds with your savings he should not be punished. You see, he really has helped you. You might have withdrawn your money and purchased an automobile. With this automobile you might have been injured in a wreck. Therefore, he who steals your money should be hailed as a protecting friend.)

"Fantastic! No one in his right senses would fall for such ridiculous twisting of reason and fact," you protest. Well, an additional illustration may convince you that it is not quite so fantastic as it would seem to be.

Sheldon and Eleanor Glueck presented the findings of the most detailed and most nearly objective study of delinquency ever made. In *Unravelling Juvenile Delinquency*, they demonstrated beyond all reasonable doubt that theories which constituted the source of the vision as it related to criminality, were not correct. Their findings showed that no significant relationship existed between economic deprivation and criminality, between strict parental discipline and criminality, or between any of the other pseudo-scientific "causes" which form a basis of the extensive programs we have adopted to prevent criminality and to reform the criminals. Other objective studies similarly fail to find that this supposed relationship actually exists.

What is the reaction of those who direct the extensive and expensive programs? Do they concede their error and change their approach? Far from it. Their first reaction is to request that the identical programs be extended! Next, they use Orwell's Reversal.

At the present time an extensive survey of juvenile delinquency is being made by the Government. This Juvenile Delinquency Project of the United States Children's Bureau is directed by one Bertram M. Beck. Newspaper accounts cite Mr. Beck's reaction to the Glueck study which effectively demolished the foundations of the jerry-built structure on which our approach to the problem of criminality is based. One of these accounts is headed: **Too**

OBEDIENT CHILD DEEMED A PROBLEM. Another account is captioned: CONFORMING CHILD SEEN AS PROBLEM. Delinquents are described as normal children by this director of a nationwide program; law-abiding children are portrayed as a threat to society! Of course he rejects the possibility that discipline and firm justice might somewhat quell the mountainous waves of criminality.

Thus, at the very highest levels, Orwell's Reversal becomes a standard part of the interpretation as we are told that actually delinquents possess many desirable traits, and led to believe that the real threat to society comes from law-abiding children; that honest children "may well be sicker than delinquents who often have no conscious guilt or anxiety."

Orwell's Reversal thus enables visionaries not only to continue their programs but to expand them in defiance of reality, and in flagrant disregard for the welfare of society.

Before passing on to a description of some of the ways in which the vision of emancipation has affected other aspects of behavior, one ironic item must be mentioned. It was in Chicago, more than fifty years ago, that a Juvenile Court was first established to mark the beginning of the new approach to criminality. Now spread throughout the Country, the approach sought to help criminals rather than to punish them, to attribute their behavior to repressions and frustrations, and to encourage them to express themselves. Recently, also in Chicago, a revolutionary new plan has been tried, and apparently with some success. On a small scale to be sure, they are now conducting an experiment in which criminal youths are put in jail! This small-scale experiment may be the first whisper that we have learned something from the tragic costs we have paid for doctrines derived from the pseudo-scientific sources of the vision of personal emancipation, as applied to our treatment of criminals.

Happily Ever After?

According to the vision, marriages would be more satisfying as well as longer-lasting once we put into practice doctrines flowing from the theories which formed its source.

We have now widely adopted the recommended courses in preparation for marriage and in sex education. Books and articles by the hundreds keep us up-to-the-minute on the techniques of courtship, marital relations, and child-rearing. Marriage counsellors and experts in domestic relations are ready to repair those rents in the fabric of domestic felicity which lead husbands and wives to the courts. In marital relationships and in sexual behavior the vision is already embodied into our practices to a degree far greater than even its most ardent proponents would have dared hope even a few short years ago. And what is this embodiment? As we strip away the glistering tinsel which wrapped this promise for the future, what substance do we find? We have surely paid enough installments at least to entitle us to glimpse what we are buying.

In 1920, when the vision was but a haze on the horizon, there were 170,000 divorces granted in the United States. In 1946, a comparable postwar year (but one in which the vision had crystallized into a guiding light for many people), there were well over 600,000 divorces granted. In both these years the number of divorces was enlarged by postwar circumstances; otherwise the contrast is valid. The figures of the number of divorces show a steady and marked upward trend, rather than the decline which was supposed to accompany our new enlightenment. Though the actual number of divorces is now lower than it was in the peak year of 1946, marriages are declining at an ever faster rate, so that the ratio between marriage and divorce is almost as unfavorable as it was in the years following the second world war.

According to present trends, almost one out of every three people who marry will terminate their marriage by divorce. Many others will separate, without going through the legal process of divorce. For full-fledged visionaries—those determined that their personalities shall not be shackled by children, by archaic traditions, or by superstitious religious restraints—some six or seven out of each ten will find themselves emancipated also from the bonds of matrimony. Meantime (despite many claims to the contrary) the marriage-rate declines. The reality of ever-increasing divorce rates combined with declines in marriage-rates indicates that also for marriage the bright wrappings of the vision's promise have been concealing bitter pills of delusion.

As for sexual behavior which violates moral codes, there is no need for extensive documentation. All studies, without exception, show that such violations are increasing at an extremely rapid rate. Pre-marital sexual relations, adultery, homosexuality, rape and other forms of promiscuous sexual behavior increase rapidly at the very time when more courses in sex education, more books and articles on the subject, more counsellors, function to "eliminate ignorance".

Veils of mystery were removed from sex, gently at first and hesitatingly. Earlier devotees of the vision made moderate requests, pleading merely for factual information to bring about some decrease in feminine inhibitions. With the passage of time they grew increasingly bold. Some now make the outright recommendation that youths "let their glands be their guides", while others gleefully proclaim, "Next, we shall teach techniques."

[74]

Professor Kinsey, in his volume on female sexual behavior, repeatedly stresses how desirable it is for females to engage in sexual relations before they are married. Referring to the "scientific proof" of Kinsey's findings, a prominent clergyman, writing in *Sex Life of the American Woman and the Kinsey Report,* indicates that we should abandon the ethics which governed adherence to our traditional moral codes and revise them around Professor Kinsey's findings.

As we nibble on the strange fruit from the tree which flourishes on the noxious sap of scientism, we might well pause to note how its shadow casts a pall upon the flower of maidenhood. Rigid and more demanding standards which formerly governed the conduct of women now decline at a rate more rapid than those of men. Though women are still restricted from doing some things which men are permitted to do, and though condemnation of female violations is still somewhat more severe than that directed at males, these differences decrease and become more difficult to distinguish. When the veils of mysticism are removed, to make sex solely a physiological process, romanticism loses its charm; as women lower their standards to approach those of men, special treatment in the form of chivalry, respect and courtesy, dissipates.

According to the vision, even such undesirable results would be relatively unimportant because, as women became emancipated from their rigid codes and were no longer "conditioned" against sex, husbands and wives would make better marital adjustments. Despite great expansion in the program, despite great increases in pre-marital sexual experimentation on the part of women, this aspect of the vision is also a delusion. An indirect measure of this delusion is found in the large number of divorces.

Nor do direct measures bear out the promise, though the data are scanty. Increases in adultery, particularly among people with college educations, is one indication that perfect marital adjustment is far from a reality. Even this condition does not reveal the full extent of the trend. For, limited though the evidence is, it seems that as sex education increases, as pre-marital experimentation flourishes, as virtually all forms of sexual behavior increase apace, one honored form declines. Sexual relations between husbands and wives (instead of increasing to promote "better adjustment") actually seem to *decrease,* decade by decade!

Orwell's Reversal is also employed by visionaries who find that their doctrines about marriage are associated with aggravation of the very conditions which they are supposed to ameliorate or cure. As divorce rates increased, the extent and gravity of the increase was at first denied. Finally, when the magnitude of divorce became so great that it could no longer be denied, it was asserted that divorce was a good thing after all. Thus some of the visionaries claim (without substantial evidence) that increasing divorce rates are proof that the American family is being *reorganized—not* disorganized!

A practicing attorney, writing in the same book as the minister who contended that moral codes should be revised in accordance with Professor Kinsey's findings, proclaims that

> . . . the most encouraging note about the new Kinsey report is its indication that more and more women are beginning to commit more and more sex crimes . . . *(P. 183)*

Again we find ourselves in the upside-down world of *1984* as lawyers applaud criminality—instead of prosecuting criminals. Professor Kinsey himself contributes an interesting reversal when he contends that adults who sexually molest children, rather than harming the child may actually help him by contributing to his "socio-sexual development". The real offenders in such cases, according to Professor Kinsey, are those who become angered over such molestations, *i.e.*, the parents.

If you ask, "Is there no end, no limit, to this nonsense?" the answer must be given as a decided "No!" Only a few years ago Professor Kinsey shocked some people by contending that homosexuality, as well as all other forms of sexual behavior, was normal. He implied that such practices are even somewhat "more normal" than those which conform with moral codes, though he did not state it. Within a few years, however, some writers took the next step and placed the blame on non-homosexuals because they criticize such practices. Others now proclaim that these sexual perverts are the real hope of free speech and democracy!

Data could be cited to show the widespread increases in dope-addiction, wholesale cheating in examinations by college students, and other practices which prevail to an extent which would shock our forefathers. Visionaries would be quick to contend that nothing new characterizes the current scene, and would point out that crime, immorality, and graft existed throughout history. In criticism of my portrayal of the present as a time when perverted theories exert undue influence, they could point to similar theories of the past—and properly so.

In his scholarly analysis, *The Conservative Mind*, Russell Kirk refers to a letter in which the great Irish-born statesman, Edmund Burke, more than 150 years ago observed that even then philosophers (in order to insinuate atheism into young minds) would "flatter all their passions natural and unnatural [and] explode or render odious or contemptible . . . virtues which restrain the appetite."

When their disciples are thus left free and guided only by

present feeling they are no longer to be depended upon for good or evil. The men who today snatch the worst criminals from justice will murder the most innocent persons tomorrow. *(P. 29)*

Thus from Burke we see that the tenets of the vision are not modern, that those who claim it to be the shiny-new product of science demonstrate not only their lack of understanding of science but also their denial of philosophy and of history. "Minute philosophers", they were called by Bishop Berkeley as in almost perfect detail he long ago described the more zealous of such visionaries who contended then as they do now

... that there is no God or providence; that man is as the beasts that perish; that his happiness, as theirs, consists in obeying animal instincts, appetites, and passions; that all stings of conscience and sense of guilt are prejudices and errors of education ... that vice is beneficial to the public ... to erase the principles of all that is great and good from the mind of man, to unhinge all order of civil life, to undermine the foundations of morality, and, instead of improving and ennobling our natures, to bring us down to the maxims and ways of thinking of the most uneducated and barbarous nations, and even to degrade human kind to a level with brute beasts. *(P. 357)*

Contrasts with the Past

Despite the fact that vice has always been with us, and though we can call up from the past statements which describe the tenets of what we today call "modern social science", the reality is now fundamentally different from what it was in bygone days.

Previously, such views were limited. They were expressed by a small number of philosophers, and the comparatively few people who read their works read also the works of other philosophers, the majority of whom opposed such ideas.

In the past such ideas were not only in the minority, they could be accepted or rejected on philosophical grounds. Now, not only are such ideas to be found in the majority of "social science" books but, with increased schooling, their audience is vastly more great. Most importantly, their influence is now strengthened by the exalted prestige of science—strengthened to a degree which makes difficult their rejection; which subjects even those who make valid criticism to the charge: "anti-scientific"! Thus, in addition to reaching a mass audience instead of a limited group, the ideas are now sheltered by the prestige of science in a manner which protects them from the open air of controversy. To cite

Irving Babbitt, "the busybody, for the first time perhaps in the history of the world, has been taken at his own estimate of himself."

Public apathy is another (and in my judgment highly significant) difference which makes the present situation distinctively different from that of the past. One "Scarlet Letter" created a scandal which shocked an entire community; one alleged sports fix (the "Black Sox" scandal) shook the entire Country; one case of graft (Teapot Dome) ruined careers and reverberated through years of political history. Now we are likely to be amused rather than shocked when we hear of scandal. The most flagrant offenses are quickly forgotten, and excuses are found to justify the conduct of those involved. Of course evil existed in earlier days but, unlike the present, people recognized it as such, called it by name, and were aroused by it to righteous indignation. Now, in accordance with the "new morality", we glorify ourselves as being "tolerant" or "broadminded". We no longer demonstrate a capacity for moral indignation.

Indeed, in the increasingly wider employment of Orwell's Reversal, we are extolling vice and condemning virtue. Non-criminals become almost a more serious problem than criminals; divorce becomes an indication of marital reorganization; chastity is looked upon as a handicap to marriage; and those who uncover subversives and traitors are condemned more vehemently than are the traitors themselves.

Unique also to the current scene is the notion of *statistical morality*. This modern invention, an offshoot of the obsession for statistics which possesses many of the zealots of scientism, has been stressed most strongly by Professor Kinsey. It is also expressed by others. Somehow (according to statistical morality), if a sufficient number of people engage in practices which violate moral codes, the behavior becomes "normal", not immoral. Thus, according to the doctrine, all forms of sexual practice are normal if either enough people engage in them or if lower animals behave similarly. We see another expression of statistical morality when governmental administrators shrug off widespread subversion and console us with the information that only one percent or only three percent of the officers of government were involved. Perhaps we must wait until fifty-one percent of governmental employees are found to be subversive (or "risks") before we consider the situation to be serious.

A fundamental fallacy in the statistical concept of morality is a failure to appreciate that moral standards are ideals which never have been, and by their very nature probably never will be, completely attained. Perhaps this vital element in ideals can be explained best by analogy: Our ideal is physical health. We know that many people are sick, but we do not, because of this statistical fact, forsake our attempts to stay healthy. Many persons are neurotic or psychotic, but this fact does not lead us to abandon our ideal of sanity.

Parents may prefer to bring up their children in accordance with statistical realities, but most of them still sense that it is preferable to rear their families according to the admittedly "unrealistic" ideals of honesty.

Fallacies of "The New Morality"

Tolerance, internationalism, slum clearance, living wages, pacifism and other elements embodied in the new morality also fail when measured as moral principles. Adherence to such beliefs requires no appreciable sacrifice. It constitutes no test of character. Most such tenets involve a position wherein you affirm *your* righteousness by demanding that *someone else* do something.

It is comfortable and pleasant to raise your voice against slums so long as you personally—and directly—do not have to pay for the improvements. Your character is tested in relation to "low wages" only if you yourself are an employer and make a significant sacrifice by raising wages. Pacifists, presumably, believe themselves moral—but they are not renouncing anything because they never did have the power to start wars. And as has been said before, it is always possible that they "mistake their fear for virtue".

Like the vision, the new morality which encircles it is largely a delusion and a perversion. As we pause to look at reality we find that what we hoped to be an upward path leading us to new horizons of enlightenment is actually a slope down which we insensibly slide into a spiritual and ethical pit.

Long ago Lord Macauley, one of the keenest observers of the tendencies inherent in our way of life, predicted that one day in some season of adversity we would devour our seedcorn. In truth, it seems that we are trampling our moral and spiritual tradition—in a frantic quest after the vision of emancipation.

Chapter V

The Maxims: Rules of Life

To COMPREHEND the acts of man without thinking of his behavior in a social context is as
difficult as are attempts to understand fish without water to swim
in, birds without air in which to fly. Forms of life and their behavior can be understood only in relation to the natural environment within which they normally function. It is natural for a bird
to fly; it is a travesty for a worm to do so. It is natural for a fish
to spend most of its life beneath the water, but a cat which
prowled around in the depths would be an abnormal feline indeed. It is natural for man to live with his fellows in societies,
though such inter-dependent relationships would be strange behavior for bears and tigers.

When fish are stranded on the beach they die, and though on
occasion some species of fish may leap through the air, though
salmon in their frantic struggle to spawn may wriggle over stret-
ches of land, even these seeming departures from natural environment can only be understood in relation to it. Birds hop along the
ground, and they do make nests in trees, but such behavior does
not lead people to confuse them with either squirrels or frogs.
Similarly, though human beings may fly through the air in planes,
and remain for days submerged in submarines they are neither
birds nor fish. Though hermits may live for years in solitude, and
even gregarious persons occasionally seek escape from the companionship of their fellows, man is unavoidably a social being.
Not only is it impossible to comprehend human behavior apart

from its natural environment within a social context, but conclusions from studies which ignore this fundamental relationship give us portrayals which are superficial and misleading.

At the other extreme, those studies which portray civilized man as the puppet of his social environment, as a creature who is unwittingly and completely molded by his culture, are as efforts to describe birds by analyzing the ingredients of the atmosphere, or fish by separating the hydrogen and oxygen which make up water.

For even limited comprehension, some balance needs be struck between the relative influences of innate tendencies which drive men to action, which in their varying intensity distinguish men one from another, and cultural influences which act as cohesive forces to bind their diversities into similar patterns of behavior within each society. No one knows where this balance lies, and an accurate description of human behavior in civilized society is a dream rather than a reality.

For our purposes, we shall emphasize some of the cultural elements, some of the social rules of life which are essential to society and which are either grotesquely distorted or blissfully ignored by those who are obsessed by the vision of personal emancipation.

Social Controls

No lengthy study of human civilizations is needed to understand the obvious: That for each man to vent every whim, to give full and complete expression to all of his passions of hate, lust and fear, is to plunge mankind to brute-level. It is readily clear that in some measure at least, people must control their emotions and respect the rights of others. Questions do arise about the degree to which individual desires should be subordinated to the social welfare, and a clearer understanding of civilized life might be reached if the nature of these restraints on individual desires —the *social controls*—is described.

Social controls include a pattern of pressures which a society exerts upon its members to maintain order within the society; to promote predictability of relationships between the people of the society; and to insure the continuance of the society. The need to preserve some degree of order within the society requires no elaboration, but the role of social controls in promoting predictability of relationships and insuring continuance of the society might be less immediately clear.

Unless you are unusually brave or unusually phlegmatic, chills would probably run up and down your spine if you were to find yourself in the midst of a group of inmates at a mental institution.

You may have read that most mentally disordered patients are not violent, or an attendant may have assured you that there was absolutely no danger, yet it is likely that you would feel quite disturbed, nevertheless. You sense that the inmates' behavior is not predictable—that at any moment one of them might decide that you are the hated enemy who tortures his twisted brain. Deprived of predictability, we feel uncertainty, disquietude, even stark fear.

Predictability is one of a class of things so important to our lives, yet taken so much for granted, that we ordinarily overlook its ever-present importance. Consider for a moment the state of confusion we would be in were we to board a train for New York only to be taken to Kansas City because the engineer decided that he was tired of going to New York; if waiters brought what they felt was good for us instead of what we ordered; if firemen poured gasoline on our burning homes; if nobody kept appointments; if stores opened whenever the whim occurred to their managers, and if prices depended on the mood of clerks. Predictability is an essential element in social relations, and one function of social controls is to maintain it.

The continuance of the society, like the necessity to preserve order, should be an axiomatic factor in social conduct. Yet even some college students question this, apparently believing that millennia of human civilization were designed to culminate in their own personal pleasure. A proper rebuttal to those who question the necessity for perpetuating the society is to suggest to them that it is unfortunate that their parents did not feel likewise!

A variety of pressures operates to preserve order, to further predictability of relationships and to perpetuate the society. For descriptive purposes these pressures are classified as formal controls and informal controls. Formal social controls include civil statutes, criminal codes and the machinery (police, courts, prisons) to enforce them. Though the formal controls are important, they cannot function effectively unless they are reinforced by the informal controls.

Folkways and Mores

One of the first sociologists in the United States, William Graham Sumner, made a useful distinction between two types of informal controls by using the terms *folkways* and *mores*. During the course of experience acquired by a society, ways of doing things will be discovered which are more effective than other ways. These are the folkways. To eat pie with a fork, to shake hands when introduced, to dress according to the occasion—these are folkways. They give rise, as Sumner observed, to habit in the individual and to custom in the group. To violate the folkways is usually no crime, but violators are looked upon as eccentric or ill-bred. There is nothing intrinsically evil in eating pie with your fingers, and you will not be arrested if you wear one sneaker and one shoe, but social controls in the form of ridicule or scorn lead most people to conform in such behavior.

Folkways differ from place to place, from group to group, and they change from time to time. Some folkways of New Yorkers differ from those of people in New England, and both differ from those of people in the Southern Appalachians. Modes of dress and speech change with time, going from crinoline to blue jeans, from silk stockings to zoot-suits. A woman who wore high heels, lip rouge and mascara, who dyed her hair, who smoked and drank in public, would have been instantly labeled as a loose woman in the past. Need further words be added to show how much the folkways change?

Mores, though unwritten, exert a powerful social influence. They include a judgment that certain behavior threatens the basic order or continuance of the society. Robbery, rape, larceny, murder, premarital sexual relations, adultery and perversions were breaches of the *mores.* Such behavior also violated formal social controls as embodied in legal statutes, but *mores* differ from these. They contain a large element of faith and sentiment, while laws are more rational and mechanical. Laws, no matter how carefully detailed, soon lose their effect when no longer buttressed by the *mores. Mores* must be ingrained and deeply felt, else they lose their controlling power. To attempt to make the *mores* rational, to alter them to fit each separate case of violation, is not to "improve" the *mores* but, according to Sumner, is similar to an attempt to reorganize the earth by redistributing the elements in it.

Yet *mores* also change with the years. If the *mores* require immediate and strong emotional reaction against violators, as Sumner contended, vast changes have occurred in their composition. Public reaction to acts which formerly constituted violations of the *mores* becomes less pronounced, more tenuously rationalistic. We tend to see each violation as an exception, and the exceptions go on to become the rule.

Earlier, I indicated how our reactions to violations—whether they involve sex, robbery, murder, or even treason—become more and more rationalistic. Instead of reacting with righteous indignation we seek excuses to explain the behavior. In so doing, we consider ourselves to be tolerant, sophisticated, rational. We may, however, be reflecting our apathy and lack of intestinal fortitude. Conscious of our own violations and of our own temptations to behave similarly, we may excuse offenders with a vague presentiment that should we be caught we may get off lightly too. We find excuses for criminals in terms of the poverty of their parents, ignoring the fact that our grandparents lived lives of rectitude in poverty far more drastic. It is not remarked that we are reversing the proverb so as to make the sins of the parents the reward of their children. As H. L. Mencken sagely observed, even murderers are now presumed innocent until proved insane!

Moral indignation dissolves in the acids of rationalism, the behavior is then looked upon as "normal", and finally we employ Orwell's Reversal to make it even better than normal. In all seriousness it can be asked, of educated people in particular: "What now remains in the *mores?*"

The Ethos

Though folkways differ from place to place, they do have a strain of consistency. Underneath the surface diversity of society lies the *ethos*, a pattern of related beliefs which gives the society its distinctive characteristics and which determines the direction and rate of social changes. Unfortunately, like so many other vitally significant aspects of civilized society, the constituent parts of the *ethos* are intangible and impossible to describe precisely.

Some contend that materialism is the most distinguishing feature of the American *ethos,* and our zeal to acquire mechanical gadgets would seem to support this contention. Yet no country has given such unselfish assistance to others in their times of trouble as has our own.

We say that we believe in equality, yet the feeling seems to be more nearly one in which we believe ourselves as good as anyone above us but better than those beneath. So, too, we believe in "democracy"—but with important reservations. In comparison with most other societies we do seem to venerate education and science in high degree, to stress individual worth more than family background and, more than others, to apply the pragmatic test ("Never mind how good it sounds. Does it work?") to our affairs. More than others we also appear to value fairness, openness, frankness.

Within a matrix of the *ethos*, folkways and *mores* of the past interwove into a pattern of social control which all but idiots comprehended. Violators, for the most part, were fully aware of their guilt, and conforming citizens were not ashamed to designate violations as evil. Yet the situation, I am sure, never was one in which people were molded completely by the forces of culture or one in which they were the helpless victims of their unconscious desires, as the pseudo-scientific theories which constitute the source of the vision would have us believe.

More nearly descriptive of past conditions, as well as of those of the present, is a view in which individual desires interact with cultural social controls.

Individual Desires and Social Controls

The modern view, on which so much of our educational effort and so many of our child-rearing practices are based, assumes that social controls directly conflict with individual desires. While it is true that during our lifetime we all restrain some desires, our submission is not usually a blind, bovine conformity but a sensed sacrifice of personal pleasure for social good. Even from the viewpoint of an individual himself, such restraints constitute small present loss for future reward in the form of self-respect and a fuller life.

Rather than view the social controls as dogmatic and arbitrary demands which stifle, suppress and frustrate individual desires, it may be more meaningful to think of them as rules-of-the-game —as channels for the direction of energy, rather than as barriers to its expression. Though such rules may require that present pleasure be renounced, postponement rather than abandonment is usually involved. In other cases one aspect of happiness lost is compensated for by another which is gained. Postponement often adds zest to the pursuit and gives full flavor to the joy of attainment.

Nor are the individual desires unyielding in their imperious demand for full and immediate release. The behavior of people in society can be better understood through an appreciation of the differences which exist within the framework of their similarities than by an assumption that they are identical. The degree of force behind individual drives, and the very nature of the drives themselves, differs appreciably from one person to another.

People differ, and such differences affect both the manner and the degree to which culture impinges upon their behavior. Some are strong and vigorous, with an excess of animal energy; others are weak and indolent. Some are highly intelligent and possess an insatiable curiosity; others are dull and disinterested. Some are brave and venturesome to the point of foolhardiness; others are cautious or timid. People differ in the rate at which they mature, and in the degree of their maturity. Men differ in many significant respects from women. Different degrees and different types of individual drives exist, but in all cases they may be thought of as flexible and adjustable in relation to the social controls rather than as rigid and unyielding in their adamant opposition to them.

To suppose (as do the theories which constitute the source of the vision) that the social controls of a culture are as steel bands which relentlessly and inflexibly squeeze everyone into the identical mold; to suppose that the rigid shafts of individual desires are broken as they strike against this impenetrable armor is, in my opinion, a misleading approach to an understanding of the rules of life in civilized society. To add to these suppositions the unproved hypothesis that, when shattered by the social controls, pieces of these shafts of individual desire fall into the smoldering fires of an unconscious mind which years later ejects them as uncontrolled emotional outbursts, is distortion rather than description.

The Behavioral Environment

In an attempt to understand our motivations and the nature of the social controls which preserve order, promote predictability of behavior, and insure continuance of the society, it seems to me more enlightening to think of both the motives and the controls as adaptable rather than as being rigid.

Not all aspects of culture are imposed with equal force on each segment of the diverse personalities upon which they fall. To live under the influence of a given culture is not to lie in a Procrustean bed where each is stretched longer or cut shorter to fit exactly the measurements of his environment. Cultural influences act upon us, but we react to them selectively rather than indiscriminately. Rather than an undifferentiated, all-encompassing, all-powerful culture pressing with equal weight upon all aspects of the personality of each person, we can think of both the cultural controls and the individual drives as being selective as well as adaptable—of a *behavioral* environment, as Kurt Koffka designates it in his *Principles of Gestalt Psychology*.

We need only consider a few of the differences between people to grasp the significance of thinking in terms of behavioral environment rather than in terms of an hypothetical culture which compresses uniform desires into uniform molds.

To persons who are tone-deaf, music is an aspect of culture which has little meaning. To those otherwise endowed it is an important manner of expression. Colors of clothing and furnishings are matters of much concern to those endowed with keen perception, as women generally are. For the color-blind, this element of culture is entirely different. Participation in athletics is a cultural outlet for those endowed with strength, stamina, and good reflexes. The less fortunately equipped can view the games, and approve or deride, but for them this aspect of culture has different meaning. Drinking may be a casual social gesture for some; to an alcoholic it is the essence or curse of life. Our temperament and our emotional stability strongly influence the impact of culture upon each one of us. Some are able to adapt themselves with equanimity to war or poverty, national catastrophe or personal loss. Others become upset and excited over minor happenings. They live their lives, according to the apt description of Professor Arnold Green, "perpetually teetering on the edge of a one-foot precipice."

According to our different endowments and predispositions each of us reacts differently and selectively to various aspects of the culture. Within the general *milieu*, each has his own behavioral environment in which he, through his interpretation, modifies the culture as well as being modified by it.

Controls: Artificial Deterrents, or Natural Rules?

When, as in the past, social controls were well-defined and comprehended they may have been stimulants to endeavor rather than suppressors of it. A case could be made—and I believe it would be essentially correct—to the effect that firm rules help, rather than hinder, individual expression. Whereas the theories from which arises the vision of emancipation would lead us to believe that social controls stifled expression, a different version of the situation may have at least equal validity.

We cannot judge excellence, adequacy or failure in human endeavors without definite rules. This maxim we take for granted in most of our pursuits, and it is at our peril that we attempt to evade it. In sports; in football, basketball, boxing, we cannot judge performance except as we assess it in terms of definite rules of the game. We judge carpenters, bricklayers, doctors and lawyers by standards which are set for their performance. With some endeavors, such as politics or religion, many intangibles prevent a clear defining of the rules, but do not eliminate their existence. Such rules not only give meaning to our efforts, not only enable us and others to weigh our attainments, they provide a spur. They enable us to fix our sights and to measure our progress.

Commenting on this theme, Solomon Asch, in his *Social Psychology*, observes that we confuse our understanding of human behavior when we assume that social controls distort personality; when we suppose that "real" human personality is revealed only when behavior is stripped of "inhibitions". He contends that adherence to some standards of social control is an integral part of the human make-up, just as real and important as are individual desires:

Why not seize the horns of the dilemma and say that it is

[87]

part of human nature itself to take measures to control and direct its own tendencies? Men are willing to adopt procedures to curb their one-sided and temporary desires in the light of steadier aims that are also theirs. They are capable of creating barriers to their own impulses; the barriers are part of them as much as the impulses. . . .   *(Pp. 352-3)*

Social controls—the rules of life—can be thought of as an outgrowth of human tendencies which are just as real as are desires for selfish individual expression. In this purview social controls need not be considered as rigid regulations which conflict with "natural" tendencies, to inhibit and distort them, but as self-created channels through which our urges may flow with least harm to others and with greatest long-term benefit to ourselves.

There will be occasions in every life when deep-felt desires will have to be postponed or permanently restrained, and there will always be persons whose willfulness prevents them from conforming. Yet we profit from definite rules for behavior, not only from the needs of an ordered society but also from a yearning for the fuller satisfaction of earned attainment. Both from a standpoint of rounded development and from the perspective of societal needs, the role of social controls can be better understood as performing larger functions even as they temporarily inhibit "natural" expression. Such rules provide channels wherein the force of expression, resulting though it does from an impetus supplied by individual desire (but deriving its very meaning from a cultural context), can flow more smoothly and more deeply. As steam generated by the fires of desire can be wastefully or harmfully expended, or by its control converted to useful purpose, so social controls can contribute to individual happiness as well as to societal purposes.

This interpretation of social controls as a positive and constructive influence on human behavior was well expressed by Charles H. Cooley in *Human Nature and the Social Order,* where he states:

> All good citizens want the laws to be definite and vigorously enforced, in order to avoid the uncertainty, waste and destruction of a lawless condition. In the same way right-minded people want definite moral standards, enforced by general opinion, in order to save the mental wear and tear of unguided feelings.   *(P. 256)*

Dissipation of Social Controls

No longer do the social controls serve to stimulate and to guide our behavior into safe channels as they did in the past. One reason for this weakening of the guiding influence of the controls is found in urbanization and mobility, as described earlier. Urban living is conducive to evasion of controls. Our high rates of mobility enable us to escape social pressures which otherwise would tend to restrain the expression of self-centered individual desires. Under such conditions the pressures of ridicule, scorn and ostracism which formerly reinforced social controls lose their force as restraining influences on behavior.

More basic and more influential than urbanization and mobility, however, is the influence of scientism. Theories, seemingly scientific, persuaded visionaries that our traditional standards of behavior were artificial and rigid. Many humanitarian persons were led to believe that individual drives and desires were inherently good, that their "natural" functioning was suppressed and frustrated by the social controls. The situation was envisioned as a direct conflict between artificially restrictive controls and natural tendencies toward emancipated goodness. Out of such conflict, the theories contended, came warped personalities, and these were subject to emotional disturbances in their sex life, in their marital relations, and in their influence upon children. Individual expression was exalted and restraints imposed by social controls were looked upon as "unnatural", due to such scientistic descriptions.

As these doctrines spread; as they are implemented in educational practices, in the treatment of criminals, in marital relations and in the manner of raising children, we find indolence, ineptitude and vandalism among school pupils and soaring rates of criminality and divorce. Such conditions were described in "The Reality", and will be summarized later in this chapter, but I would like first to make a few observations about a less obvious aspect of our changing relationships.

Breakdown of Role Relationships

Predictability of behavior was described as one of the functions performed by the social controls. An understanding of the roles fulfilled by people under various circumstances is an important element in predictability.

Though some overlapping existed, and though few people were completely consistent, a high degree of role fulfillment generally prevailed in the past. Husbands had one role, wives another. Certain rules of conduct were followed by elders, others by children. Teachers and pupils generally understood and respected the different behavior required by their respective roles. The confusion and uncertainty which now characterizes role relationships is one aspect of the general loss of clarity in social

[89]

controls. In some instances this uncertainty is apparent upon observation, in others it can only be indirectly inferred.

Observe the comic strips and radio or television programs which deal with contemporary relations between husbands and wives. Almost without exception, husbands are portrayed as amiable but blustering and undignified clowns whose principal contribution to the marital relationship is wiping dishes. Wives are tolerant, foresighted and wise rulers of the household and guardians of their husbands' imbecilities. Children generally are depicted as having an attitude of amused condescension toward their father; of affection and understanding for their mother. Mothers are girls and fathers are pals. Soldiers are boys. Teachers are companions in the learning process as they try to lower themselves to the level of their pupils (and frequently succeed).

I do not mean to imply that perfect roles were fixed in the past and that we should never deviate from them; I am trying to point out that part of the lack of predictability in modern life is due to the uncertainty and confusion which is associated with roles no longer clearly defined. We praise these undefined roles as presaging "democracy" and companionship within family life and education, and perhaps this is the case. Perhaps an appreciable modification of the authoritarian measures which formerly were imposed by fathers and teachers has had many desirable effects on wives, children and pupils. Certainly it is pleasurable to ridicule the tyrannical, narrow-minded father or teacher whose punishment was qualified with "This hurts me more than it does you."

Salutary effects may accompany a dissolution of the unwritten rules which formerly cast fathers and teachers in their roles of strict disciplinarians. Our motive in discarding the robes of authority may be a genuine desire for tolerance and equalitarian democratic relationships. It is quite possible that this is the correct interpretation. Vandalism, delinquency, criminality, perversion and divorce may be but unfortunate yet undeserved accompaniments to our noble purpose.

The Challenge—Fortitude

A different interpretation, however, may more accurately describe the relinquishment of our roles. This interpretation is one which will be understood by most parents, and it centers on the fact that it is far more difficult to mete out merited punishment to those we love than ever it is to close our eyes to their wrongdoing.

As parents, we know that the limited experience of children, and their intense absorption in the pleasures of the moment, naturally prevent their comprehension of many rules. While adults have learned those rules which are essential to the society and beneficial in the long range of a lifetime, they know that such precepts are as unreal and preposterous to children as is the thought that *they* will some day be grandparents. So it is particularly tempting to close our eyes to infractions when we can cloak the remission of our obligations with a resplendent mask of "science"; when we can translate timorous equivocation into terms of progressive and democratic enlightenment. And thus we take an easy course, and evade responsibility.

Truer now than ever before is the observation that "The brave are lonely." Parents and teachers who were stern but just and who tempered their firmness with fairness, always needed a sizeable reserve of intestinal fortitude to aid them as they clung to their principles despite misunderstanding, ridicule, and the ever-present temptation to forsake their role and to become a "good fellow".

In earlier days, however, those who staunchly resisted temptations to temporize and who steadfastly eschewed cheaply-won plaudits for goodfellowship were fortified in their inner resolve by strong social and religious pressures. Such strong and clear-cut social and religious pressures—firm social controls—have had their foundations sapped by pseudo-scientific theories and their substance leached from them by secular rationality. Not only do social controls now fail to supplement inner resolve but increasingly we find that (as in the new morality) they now oppose it. With tolerance, rationality, moral relativism, equalitarianism and similar elements of the new morality exalted to empyrean heights as virtues, the insidious appeal of Orwell's Reversal gnaws upon our conscience to make us wonder if anything is really abnormal and leads us to speculate that "bad" is perhaps even somewhat better than "good".

We find ourselves in an ethical upside-down position as, coupled with an exaltation of moral relativism, we see firmness of character condemned as bigotry, narrow-mindedness, mid-Victorianism, and dogmatism. When we feel that we should adhere to firm moral principles derived from our religion, from our personal experience and from knowledge of the past (or perhaps even from vague hunches or intuitions), we are beset by doubts, and become hesitant and apologetic. No longer do we derive nourishment for our resolve from an invigorating moral climate. Now, inner resolve requires intestinal fortitude to a degree far greater than in the past, for otherwise the chilling winds of adverse comment blow through our arid moral climate to unstick our resolution. We no longer find firm support for our resolve in the social controls.

[91]

Today's moral challenge requires us to actively *oppose* a social climate which hinders rather than helps our inner resolve.

Different Effects of the Challenge

Theories of human behavior which assumed an innate naturalness of individual desires and stressed the artificially restraining influence of the folkways and *mores,* resulted in a weakening of the social controls. Once-clear and definite guideposts for behavior, and safe channels for the flow of our energies, they fade now into increasing vagueness. Areas in which we can behave without social censure have been widely enlarged. Barriers between socially acceptable behavior and breaches of the *mores* are lower, and they are obscured in a fog of uncertainty. Most of us have both the opportunity and the temptation to engage in a far wider variety of behavior than ever before. These temptations and opportunities conspire to encourage excursions into vaguely defined moral areas, and as we do so different effects occur depending upon our training and upon our innate stability.

To clarify the current moral situation we can think of it in terms of its contrasting influence on three different groups of people. Among us still are many older citizens who in their youth were thoroughly indoctrinated with firm principles of social control. Of the same general category would be persons who, raised in rural areas or within devoutly religious families, continue to have firm principles instilled into their character. Such people, with their view of life focused in a former perspective, are less likely than others to be aware of the many opportunities and less likely to be susceptible to the temptations. Yet even for these citizens the challenge is more demanding than it was in the past.

A second group is fortunate enough to be endowed with an inherently stable disposition. Probably equipped with a well-balanced set of endocrine glands, they sense the permissible limits of the social controls, even though these be vaguely defined. Such fortunate persons can take advantage of the wider opportunities and with reasonable safety engage in many types of behavior which were condemned in the past. Even with those of this second group, however, it is questionable that the greater variety of instant pleasures results in deeper general happiness.

It is primarily from a third group that the vandals, criminals, sex delinquents, perverts and divorced persons are drawn to crowd the current scene. Most people (including many who are convinced of their own innate stability) have potential weaknesses. In one way or another—some in relation to sex, some in relation to alcohol, others in their overweening vanity—flaws exist in our characters. In earlier times most such deficiencies were bound by the firm though elastic ties of social controls. Now, increasingly, the weaknesses find expression in ways which create unhappiness in the person and harm to others in society. This increasing group, heretofore restrained by the pressures of convention, now is tempted to embark upon excursions into vaguely defined moral areas. Lacking stability, and no longer aided by familiar guideposts, they pass the emotional or social "point of no return". Encouraged by the unprecedented opportunity and temptation which is fostered by the vision of emancipation, they are the principal products—the reality—of the vision itself.

So, what of ourselves? What of our society?

No longer fortified and guided by firm folkways and *mores*, living in an atmosphere which condemns rather than praises moral indignation and character, we attempted to enhance our stature by striking noble poses of rectitude—and we foisted responsibility upon others.

We sought for a panacea in the vision of personal emancipation, and we found that the soothing drug could not permanently still the effects of the cancer on our conscience. We sought, and we failed. And perhaps in some measure our failure is explained by an anonymous versifier whom Irving Babbitt cites in his *Democracy and Leadership:*

> And so I hold it is not treason
> To advance a simple reason
> For the sorry lack of progress we decry.
> It is this: instead of working
> On himself, each man is shirking,
> And trying to reform some other guy. *(P. 197)*

Thus we are met with today's challenge—the need for a larger measure of inner resolution, a deeper degree of intestinal fortitude. This is a challenge to each of us. And as each of us responds, so goes the future.

Part III

The Collective Quest: Security

Chapter VI

The Vision: Planned Utopia

Out of seemingly scientific theories a vision arises to convince many most sincere persons that our behavior and our beliefs should be emancipated. Doctrines flowing from pseudo-scientific sources persuade many of our people that we not only can but should free our thinking from supernatural influence, from traditional moral beliefs, from precepts gained by centuries of civilized history, and from the lessons we learn through our own experience. The promise is that we shall be able to adjust to real-life situations in a rational manner once we have cleansed our brain of such traditions, of "the heavy weight of the dead hand of the past".

I have tried to emphasize some of the fallacies inherent in the theories from which the vision of personal emancipation arises and to stress some of the harmful results which are associated with the adoption of its doctrines. Now I shall try to describe those characteristics of the vision which relate to our collective life; to portray the nature of the source from which it springs; to stress the hazards associated with the doctrines which emerge from it; and to suggest alternatives.

As it relates to our collective affairs—to the institutions associated with the operation of the Government and the functioning of the economy—the vision is outlined less clearly than that which has dazzled those who would emancipate our personal conduct. Much more complex than the behavior of an individual are the multifarious activities performed by people in their social relations, and my attempt is therefore limited to an analysis of only one aspect of our social scene. I shall try, in the following pages, to describe the influence of utopian ideas and doctrines. More specifically, after sketching the background of philosophical utopianism, the analysis will concentrate upon differences between earlier utopian schemes and those of the present, and it will particularly stress the influence of the notion of "scientific" social planning.

In relation to the vision of emancipation it was pointed out that ideas similar to those embodied in current doctrines were advanced by philosophers centuries ago. Though the system of ideas—the ideology—is not new, the present situation differs from the past in terms of the mass-audience which such ideologies reach, and the way in which the prestige of science both promotes their acceptance and shelters them from critical analysis. As the personal quest for unfettered freedom found expression in visions of emancipation, so the collective quest for security has long been expressed in visions of a Utopia.

The courses of the individual quest for emancipation and of the collective quest for security both trace back to springs which well from deep within humanity. But each ran its course in minor rivulets, separated from the flow of the broad rivers of civilization by the rocks of reality. Then came the freshets of popularized scientism. The rivulets burst their banks and plunged into the mainstream. Now we ignore the muddy cross-currents which flow from their turbulent intrusion and fix our delighted gaze on a rainbow—reflected by the spray.

Individual Utopian Proposals

From the time of the Greek philosopher Plato, many individuals have indulged their fancy in attempts to construct an imaginative ideal society. Plato called his *The Republic;* Thomas Campanella named his the *City of the Sun;* Francis Bacon's was entitled *New Atlantis;* while James Harrington labeled his *Oceana.*

Each of these differed in the basis on which the ideal society was to be founded. A description of their details would not contribute appreciably to our understanding of modern utopian influence, so brief mention will be made of only a few of the proposals. First we shall consider some of the notions of individual Utopianists, and then outline some extinct political movements of our earlier history which were tinged with utopianism.

Because his imagined society was designated by the name which is now generally applied to idealized group living, mention must be made of Sir Thomas More's *Utopia.* Robert Owen's

New Harmony will be cited also as an example of attempts to put utopian ideals into practice, while Edward Bellamy's *Looking Backward* is referred to as an illustration of the widespread appeal of utopian ideas based on economic determinism—mankind's perpetual hope that all personal and social problems can be solved by tinkering with economic processes.

Living at a time (1478-1535) when Christopher Columbus made the discovery of what he believed to be India, Thomas More's imagination was stirred. He may well have reasoned that since the discoveries of Columbus, Magellan, Vespucci and da Gama had revealed entire continents of which men never before had dreamed, similarly daring voyages of the mind might reveal entirely new and undreamed-of ways of life.

More's *Utopia* was an island where everyone, man or woman, had to work but where no one was required to labor longer than six hours per day. Education was free and universal and continued throughout life. Money was abolished. Gold and silver were molded into chamber pots or chains for slaves. Only children wore jewels, which adults scorned as baubles. Sir Thomas' conception of the perfect society, though it differs in many respects from those of others, has in common with them the beliefs that money is the root, and education the remedy, of all evil.

It may be of some significance to recall that the word "Utopia" means not-a-place, or nowhere.

Robert Owen (1771-1857), unlike most utopianists, was a highly successful man, a British industrialist. Also in contrast to others, he put into actual practice his notions of what an ideal society should be. Included among such ideas were beliefs which characterize many of the visionaries of personal emancipation: That the character of man is formed for him and not by him; that improvement of the environment will solve all human problems; that education will conquer mankind's greatest enemy, ignorance.

Owen established several of his Utopian villages in Great Britain, and in one of these (New Lanark) his principles of communal sharing functioned long enough to serve as an inspiration to Karl Marx, father of modern communism. New Harmony, Indiana, was organized according to Owen's ideas. It, like a number of other utopian projects which were put into practice in earlier American history, soon failed.

In 1887 Edward Bellamy published his version of Utopia in the form of a novel-essay, *Looking Backward*. His Utopia is described through the eyes of Julian West, who falls asleep in 1887 and does not awaken until the year 2000. All men have been made reasonable through an educational system which trains them until they are twenty-one. Their rationality has created domestic felicity and international peace. Private corporations have been supplanted by government ownership, and women as well as men are organized into an industrial army. Labor troubles, political graft, oppression, poverty and crime have all been eradicated because the new social organization fosters collectivism rather than individualism and competition. *Looking Backward* thus typifies the more recent trends in utopian beliefs.

Glenn Negley and J. Max Patrick, in their description of the more prominent Utopias (*The Quest for Utopia*), point out that Bellamy's *Looking Backward* had a greater impact on the thoughts of men than any other similar book. Well over a million copies were sold, and it has been translated into every important language. Its great and continuing popularity can be explained in terms of the twin visions: Emancipation, and Security. In pleasantly palatable fashion *Looking Backward* expressed the dream held by some visionaries then and by many now, that governmental control will solve all personal and social, as well as economic, problems.

The authors of *The Quest for Utopia* stress the manner in which utopianists shifted their focus from reform of the individual to reform of social institutions. Bellamy's imaginative description of a flawless society was illustrative of this tendency, one which becomes more pronounced as we approach the present. Like modern advocates of a planned society, Bellamy assumed that all men are essentially and fundamentally good; that evils arise solely from inequitable and inefficient social institutions, and that all major ills can be eliminated by changing the principles which govern the functioning of these institutions. Also in the modern manner, Bellamy's thesis assumed economic determinism: The belief that the economic institution is the cornerstone of the social structure.

This belief implies that all other institutions are held firmly in place by a properly constructed, strong economic organization; that if the economic organization is incorrectly shaped, the other institutions will crumble. With Bellamy—and with many modern intellectuals—economic determinism is a springboard which is used to jump to the conclusion that the major problems of society arise from inequities which are inherent in the capitalistic system. At the same time, it is commonly assumed that the problems will disappear under a collectivist economy.

Utopian imaginings, as exemplified by the ideas of Sir Thomas More, Robert Owen, Edward Bellamy and others, were primarily philosophical notions which could be accepted as reasonable or rejected as preposterous by the individuals who read them. Only Owen put his ideas into practice, and his New Harmony, like other Utopian colonies which were started at various places in the United States during our earlier history, was a brief and exotic experiment which had no appreciable influence upon our society. The proper measure of utopian writings is in terms of their influence on the beliefs of those who read about them, and by this criterion it seems that Bellamy, with his emphasis upon economic determinism, has had more effect than the others.

Practically all of the earlier philosophical utopianists portrayed their societies of the future in glowing phrases which depicted untroubled individuals living in unalloyed peace and prosperity. As time passed, at least some of the programs which were supposed to pave the way to Utopia were adopted. Universal education, looked upon as a cure for ignorance and as a lever to open the door to the happy future, became a reality. Yet surprisingly, crime, divorce and graft not only continued, they increased. Extremes between poverty and wealth decreased, but still our major problems persisted. Sensing the delusive nature of Utopian schemes, a few writers began to describe societies of the future in a manner which revealed defects in the trends of the times.

Impressed particularly by Watson's behavioristic theories of conditioning and by the tremendous technological developments of the 1920s—exemplified in the assembly-line developed by Henry Ford—Aldous Huxley wrote *Brave New World*. In Huxley's brave new world the embodiment of technological perfection (Ford) was deified as the creator of the new era. Babies were raised on bottles on an assembly-line where they were supplied with exactly the correct amount of nourishment. Since factory workers were needed for the cities, infants were subjected to strong electric shocks as they played among grass and flowers, thus conditioning them to fear life in the country. Efficiency was raised to a high level, yet the thought-control was not complete. Numbed frustration rather than happiness resulted from the "scientific" conditioning.

By 1949, when George Orwell wrote of his imagined society of 1984, techniques of the communists and of the psychoanalysts were better known. In his society of the future, Orwell depicts thought-control perfected through psychoanalytic techniques, *i.e.*, re-writing history, and brainwashing. Instead of in complete freedom, individuals dwell in complete submission to the state. The omniscient leader is "Big Brother", and the citizen's every move is observed through television recorders installed in his home. Instead of prosperity, Orwell described an extension of methods which governments even now employ to limit consumption of food through the destruction of "surpluses", and by rationing. Instead of idyllic peace there is perpetual war.

Thought-control had led all to believe that "War is Peace", and that "Freedom is Slavery".

Organized Utopian Movements

A wide variety of political movements in America were tinged with the utopian assumption that major personal and individual problems can be solved by some simple formula. A few examples of such movements illustrate that even though major elements of their doctrines have been adopted, we still are confronted by at least as many problems as we were before.

At the first national convention of the People's Party of America in 1892, the preamble of the Populist platform proclaimed:

> The newspapers are largely subsidized or muzzled, public opinion silenced, business prostrated, homes covered with mortgages, labor impoverished, and the land concentrating in the hand of capitalists. The urban workmen are denied the right to organize for self-protection, imported pauperized labor beats down their wages, a hireling standing army, unrecognized by our laws, is established to shoot them down, and they are rapidly degenerating into European conditions. The fruits of the toil of millions are boldly stolen to build up colossal fortunes for a few, unprecedented in the history of mankind; and the possessors of these, in turn, despise the Republic and endanger liberty. From the same prolific womb of governmental injustice we breed the two great classes—tramps and millionaires.

To remedy these evils, the platform recommended free and secret ballots; a graduated income tax; pensions to ex-service men; restriction of undesirable immigration; an eight-hour day in Government work; and the abolition of private police (such as those employed as strike-breakers by the Pinkerton Agency). All these measures have long since been adopted, yet the same type of complaint (though usually couched in less flaming words) is still made by the same type of people who made it then.

The year 1905 saw the Industrial Workers of the World organized as a political party. Commonly called the "Wobblies", the preamble of their 1919 platform interpreted economic problems in terms of class-struggle, in a fashion very similar to that of the Communists today:

> The working class and the employing class have nothing in common. There can be no peace so long as hunger and want are found among millions of working people and the few, who make up the employing class, have all the good things of life.
>
> Between these two classes a struggle must go on until the workers of the world organize as a class, take possession of

the earth and the machinery of production and abolish the wage system.

We find that the centering of the management of industries into fewer and fewer hands makes the trade unions unable to cope with the ever-growing power of the employing class.

Remedy was to be found in unions organized on a basis of industries instead of on the basis of crafts as was the practice in the American Federation of Labor. This element of the vision has been part of the reality of our economy since John L. Lewis established the Congress of Industrial Organizations (CIO) in the 1930s. The "Wobblies" also advocated abolition of the wage system. While we have not yet abolished wages, we have moved definitely in the direction of the "Wobblies'" goal in those industrial contracts which incorporate the idea of a Guaranteed Annual Wage.

Indirectly, but in appreciable measure, we even incorporate into our practices at least some of the measures advocated by Anarchists. Their platform is outlined in the magazine *Resistance* (September, 1947):

> That we clear our minds of the myths and superstitions we have been taught, and see the world as it actually is;
>
> That we learn to live as free people by exercising freedom and individuality in our work, our recreation, our sex and family lives, our education;
>
> That we refuse to take part in war, conquest, exploitation, imprisonment, and the other crimes of present-day society;
>
> That we join together as workers, as consumers, as victims of war and conscription, as victims of race hatred, in movements to resist the rulers' demands and to take from them the things we need;
>
> That we work together to spread the idea of freedom, to develop initiative and self-reliance, to create a society where we will be able to live as human beings.

Organized political movements such as the People's Party of America, the International Workers of the World, the Anarchists, and many others, have contained facets of the vision of security. Though many aspects of their programs have found their way into our practices, the movements themselves were short-lived and the vision remained as elusively distant as it had been before their supposed remedies were adopted. Like the philosophical notions of utopianists, such movements could either be accepted or rejected for what they were.

Not so, however, with the various forms of socialism, including communism, which borrow the prestige of science to support their economic innovations.

Socialism

As an open political movement, socialism reached the peak of its popularity in the United States soon after the first world war. Thereafter, it sharply declined. The influence of socialism cannot be measured, however, in terms of the number of people who vote for candidates of the Socialist Party. Socialistic influence, and that of communism too, is much more widespread than is indicated by party membership. The subtle and intangible influence of socialism is in the realm of ideas; ideas which arise out of exaggerated fears of the present and undisciplined hope for the future; ideas which conceal their political implications under a guise of secular humanitarianism.

According to Egbert and Persons in their history of the socialist movement, *Socialism and American Life,* the term "socialist" as a designation for tendencies toward collectivism (rather than individualism), first appeared in 1827 in a magazine published by the followers of Robert Owen. In 1890, the Socialist Party of the United States was founded. Leopold Schwarzschild, in his biography of Karl Marx *(The Red Prussian),* points out that socialists characteristically attributed limitless power to science, with each convinced that his own system established the correct scientific rules for the salvation of mankind. Most popular of the terms was "scientific socialism", coined by Pierre-Joseph Proudhon and later appropriated by Marx as the designation for communism. The promise of fulfillment of a brilliant vision was coupled with the proud prestige of science.

Socialists of various countries held forth thus in *Socialism and American Life:*

> Socialism was an unbounded dream. Fourier promised that under socialism people would be at least "ten feet tall". Karl Kautsky, the embodiment of didacticism, proclaimed that the average citizen of a socialist society would be a superman. The flamboyant Antonio Labriola told his Italian followers that their socialist-bred children would each be Galileos and Giordano Brunos. And the high-flown, grandiloquent Trotsky described the socialist millennium as one in which "man would become immeasurably stronger, wiser, freer, his body more harmoniously proportioned, his movements more rhythmic, his voice more musical, and the forms of his existence permeated with dramatic dynamism." *(P. 215)*

Down through the years, socialists proclaimed a variety of measures to implement their doctrines so as to realize their vision of cooperation, peace and economic security. In 1898 the essential features of the program adopted by the Social Democratic

Party of America were: Cooperative production and distribution; national insurance of workers against accident; elimination of the necessity for working in old age; public works to relieve unemployment; reduction of the hours of labor; equal civil and political rights for men and women; adoption of the initiative and referendum; and abolition of war through international arbitration.

Many measures included in the Socialist platform of 1898 are now incorporated into our economic and social life. The first—cooperative production and distribution—can never be politically attained since the state of mind which is most conducive to cooperation cannot be created by legislative fiat. There is, however, a large amount of cooperation which necessarily arises from the complexities of our economic system. Workers and employers, unions and management, now cooperate to a degree hardly dreamed possible in former years. Though we do not have a national insurance program to cover those who are injured at their work, the separate States have workmen's compensation acts which accomplish the same purpose. The Old Age and Survivors Insurance section of the Social Security Act provides workers with pensions. Many private businesses and industries make provisions whereby their workers receive pensions upon retirement. Extensive public works programs were adopted to relieve unemployment during the economic depression of the 1930s, and even in periods of prosperity such programs continue to operate. Hours of labor were successively reduced by the provisions of the Fair Labor Standards Act. After the end of the first world war the League of Nations was established to settle international disputes through arbitration, and following the next world war (which signalized the failure of the League) the United Nations was created for the same purpose. Of all the proposals we failed to adopt but one, the initiative and referendum, and this too was tried at times. Yet few would contend that we have by their adoption attained the ideal society envisioned in the doctrines of socialism.

Similarly we now incorporate the essence of the planks of the Socialist Party platform of 1912. This platform was prefaced by the assertion that

> It is this capitalist system that is responsible for the increasing burden of armaments, the poverty, slums, child labor, most of the insanity, crime and prostitution, and much of the disease that afflicts mankind.

The 1912 socialist recommendations for a rest period of a day-and-a-half each week are more than met by the two-day period now generally prevalent. Their demands that labor by children under 16 be forbidden and that legislation be enacted to prohibit interstate shipment of the products of child labor, have also been adopted. We have established minimum wage scales, and (in a sense at least) met their demand to abolish the profit system in government work by cost-plus contracts and by renegotiation of contracts. Socialists demanded a non-contributory system of old-age pensions, but on this issue we fall short in that, under the Social Security legislation, partial contributions are required. We have put into practice both workmen's compensation and unemployment compensation. We have also adopted (and with a vengeance) their graduated income tax and inheritance tax proposals. As for "insurance against invalidism", our State and Federal governments now spend some five billion dollars each year, an amount far in excess of that considered adequate in the wildest imaginings of the visionaries of socialized medicine in 1912.

Virtually all of the economic demands of socialists have been adopted, yet we still have slums, insanity and crime. Declines in prostitution have resulted more from amateur competition than from economic reforms. We do have an increasing burden of armaments, to be sure, but this heavy burden was itself largely brought about by two societies which themselves were socialistic. During the second world war our armaments were needed to curb the "peace-loving" tendencies of the National *Socialist* Party of Germany. Since that time we have needed them to prevent the modern fatherland of socialism—the Union of Soviet *Socialist* Republics—from engaging in "international arbitration" to a degree which could "cooperate" us out of existence.

No matter how many of their proposals were adopted, however, socialists of that time would have remained dissatisfied. For, be it noted, they concluded their 1912 list of demands with this warning:

> Such measures of relief as we may be able to force from capitalism are but a preparation for the workers to seize the whole powers of government, in order that they may thereby lay hold of the whole system of socialized industry and thus come to their rightful inheritance.

Socialists thus were distinguishable from other collectivists and social planners in that their own particular vision entailed government control of the means of production. Others who envisioned a planned society denied that their programs involved this final step in control of the society. (In the statement of principles adopted in 1951 by the Socialist delegates of 21 nations, public ownership of the means of production was omitted. In 1954, also, the Socialist Party omitted government ownership from its statement of strategy and objectives.)

Most economic changes espoused by socialists have, therefore, already been incorporated into the framework of an economy which is still designated "capitalistic". One should not infer from this that socialists or other "scientific" planners rest content upon their accomplishments. As with the visionaries of emancipation, they remain not satisfied. They never will be convinced that their program, though long since adopted in substance, fails to accomplish the wonders they envision. Concessions pave the way for further demands; the demonstrable failure of their separate projects gives rise to an insistence that the overall program be expanded. Though they now omit the demand that the society be handed over to them (through governmental control by social engineers—meaning themselves), this omission appears to be a tactical maneuver, not a change in basic strategy. This socialist tactic may have been learned from communist-front organizations, which similarly appeal to idealisms while carefully avoiding public statements of their ultimate goal.

Communism

Technically, socialism and communism differ in that communism includes governmental control of consumption as well as of production. Another point of difference involves reward for work. Theoretically, socialism would reward workers according to their productivity, communism would supply goods in accordance with need. Actually, communism, as exemplified by the Soviet, provides incentives for productivity among its workers and allows wide differences among incomes. Such differences as do exist between socialism and communism are largely theoretical; in practice their similarities far outweigh their differences. Both assume the primacy of economic determinism, and both embrace the vision of a society scientifically planned and managed by experts. Both groups of visionaries consider themselves to be the experts.

Marx carefully avoided the use of the word "communism". He did make extensive use of idealistic terms with double-meanings, designated by Lenin as "Aesopian language". The official designation for communist Russia is Union of Soviet Socialist Republics. Earl Browder, for many years top communist leader in the United States, declared:

> The program of the Socialist Party and the program of the Communist Party have a common origin in the document known as the Communist Manifesto. There is no difference, so far as the program is concerned, in final aim.

Others have compared the two by saying that "communism is socialism in a hurry".

[104]

Karl Marx (1818-1883) is the founder and patron saint of modern communism. Like most of those who, through communism or through socialism, fervently embrace the vision of security, Marx was a middle-class intellectual, not a manual worker. He was a member of the very class (the *bourgeoisie*) so despised by communists, not one of the *proletariat* which is supposed to transform the vision to reality. His collaborator and financial supporter, Friedrich Engels, was of a wealthy industrialist family. In 1848 Marx and Engels published *The Communist Manifesto,* frequently referred to as the "bible" of the communist faith. Ten steps describe the program which is supposed to lead to the Utopia:

1. Abolition of property in land and application of all rents of land to public purposes.

2. A heavy progressive or graduated income tax.

3. Abolition of all right of inheritance.

4. Confiscation of the property of all emigrants and rebels.

5. Centralization of credit in the hands of the State capital and an exclusive monopoly.

6. Centralization of the means of communication and transport in the hands of the State.

7. Extension of factories and instruments of production owned by the State; the bringing into cultivation of waste lands, and the improvement of the soil generally in accordance with a common plan.

8. Equal liability of all to labor. Establishment of industrial armies, especially for agriculture.

9. Combination of agriculture with manufacturing industries: gradual abolition of the distinction between town and country, by a more equable distribution of the population over the country.

10. Free education for all children in public schools. Abolition of children's factory labor in its present form. Combination of education with industrial production, etc., etc.

An informative summary of these programs is contained in *Organized Communism in the United States,* a pamphlet prepared by the Committee on Un-American Activities of the House of Representatives. The preamble of the 1945 constitution of the Communist Party of the United States of America is representative of such programs. As you read it, note the reference to science; observe the identification with socialism; bear in mind that in "Aesopian language" references to defending the American Constitution and its Bill of Rights mean the use of these very instruments to protect themselves until they attain power, and then to utterly destroy them. In references to "democracy", try to envision the slave-labor of the socialist-communist state. In the idealization of peace, think of peaceful Russia's self-defense against mighty, imperialistic, warlike Finland and the Baltic states. References to "democracy" and "democratic" should be interpreted with an awareness that communists do not use the terms in the same sense as do we. They refer to "democratic centralism", and it means that once the leader makes a decision, all others must agree. Since they all agree, the decision is democratic. It is even more democratic than our majority, for the agreement is unanimous. You agree—or die.

With such modifications constantly in mind, herewith is presented the 1945 Party preamble:

> The Communist Party of the United States is the political party of the American working class, basing itself upon the principles of scientific socialism, Marxism-Leninism. It champions the immediate and fundamental interests of the workers, farmers, and all who labor by hand and brain against capitalist exploitation and oppression. As the advanced party of the working class, it stands in the forefront of this struggle.

> The Communist Party upholds the achievements of American democracy and defends the United States Constitution and its Bill of Rights against its reactionary enemies who would destroy democracy and popular liberties. It uncompromisingly fights against imperialism and colonial oppression, against racial, national, and religious discrimination, against Jim Crowism, anti-Semitism, and all forms of chauvinism.

> The Communist Party struggles for the complete destruction of fascism and for a durable peace. It seeks to safeguard the welfare of the people and the nation, recognizing that the working class, through its trade unions and by its independent political action, is the most consistent fighter for democracy, national freedom, and social progress.

> The Communist Party holds as a basic principle that there is an identity of interest which serves as a common bond uniting the workers of all lands. It recognizes further that the true national interests of our country and the cause of peace and progress require the solidarity of all freedom-loving peoples and the continued and ever closer cooperation of the United Nations.

> The Communist Party recognizes that the final abolition of exploitation and oppression, of economic crises and un-

employment, of reaction and war, will be achieved only by the socialist reorganization of society—by the common owner-ship and operation of the national economy under a govern-ment of the people led by the working class.

The Communist Party, therefore, educates the working class, in the course of its day-to-day struggles, for its historic mission, the establishment of Socialism. Socialism, the high-est form of democracy, will guarantee the full realization of the right to "life, liberty, and the pursuit of happiness," and will turn the achievements of labor, science, and culture to the use and enjoyment of all men and women.

In the struggle for democracy, peace, and social progress, the Communist Party carries forward the democratic tradi-tions of Jefferson, Paine, Lincoln, and Frederick Douglass, and the great working-class traditions of Sylvis, Debs, and Ruthenberg. It fights side by side with all who join in this cause.

Both communism and socialism promise to attain the vision of security from want and war in the form of a planned Utopia. Neither, however, as an open political movement, constitutes the direct and immediate essence of the vision at the present time. The influence of each is indirect, and it is most potent as exerted by those who, entranced by their vision, do not join in open mem-bership though they espouse the essential doctrine. As moths, they flicker about the shining flame of socialism to cast the shadow of their influence upon our affairs.

Pseudo-scientific theories which give impetus to the vision of personal emancipation are amateurish and awkward, yet by the halo-glow of science they seem to brightly shine. By squinting, visionaries can shut from their sight the distorted shadows which they cast upon our lives.

The many fallacies and untested assumptions in the commu-nist and socialist bases of the vision of security enjoin their intel-lectual sympathizers from making direct and open proposals that we adopt the program. Yet they are leading us in the selfsame direction, through by-paths marked with other signs. The chal-lenge of the vision of security lies not in the blanket acceptance or rejection either of communism or of socialism; it lies in a cold and careful assessment of appeals which lead to similar ends, precisely through the by-paths marked with other signs.

These signs are enticingly labeled: Social Engineering, Social Planning, and Welfare State. All point to the highroad of col-lective security; all lead us to the chimerical promise of the vision.

So many have become aware of the jerry-built structure of socialism and now perceive that the idealistic veneer of communism is a gloss for naked oppression, that few would consciously embark on a trip which had the dream-city of socialism as its destination. Many visionaries make great show of tearing up their one-way tickets to these particular terminals. Yet their zeal to take us on such a trip is not diminished; they have changed nothing save the signposts of their ultimate destination.

They go by different routes, and designate their terminal by names which have not as yet been tarnished in the salty atmosphere of reality. Here are no appeals for us to take a journey direct to socialism; here are itineraries which lead us indirectly —to *Collectivism*, or to the *Welfare State*. The course is devious, in the Fabian manner, and the routes are designated as "social planning".

Social Planning

The *Dictionary of Modern Economics* describes collectivism as a political or economic doctrine which maintains that the ownership of property, especially of land and capital, should reside with the government. A Welfare State is a society in which the income of the individual members is determined by their needs rather than by their efforts. A similar but less popular designation is *statism*, defined by Raymond Moley in his inspiring *How To Keep Our Liberty* as

> ... a policy or philosophy that advocates a progressive trend of intervention by government in economic, social, and personal life. Those who favor such intervention will deny that state socialism is the ultimate goal of such a trend. I cannot agree with that denial. (P. xvi)

Though differences of detail exist in the types of societies designated as Communist, Socialist, Collectivist, Welfare State or Statist, they are inherently similar. Government is conceived as an agency which will directly insure economic security and thereby indirectly cure personal problems as well. Another important similarity lies in the reliance of all upon science—whether termed scientific social planning or social engineering—as a magic lever which will lift the world into the untroubled atmosphere of security from want and war.

Writing so long ago he could not foretell the vital role which scientism would play in the process, Alexis de Tocqueville in his *Democracy and America* presciently describes both the appeal and the hazards of the type of government encompassed by the vision. Such government exerts a power which

> ... is absolute, minute, regular, provident, and mild. It

would be like the authority of a parent, if, like that authority, its object was to prepare men for manhood; but it seeks on the contrary to keep them in perpetual childhood: it is well content that the people should rejoice, provided they think of nothing but rejoicing. For their happiness such a government willingly labours, but it chooses to be the sole agent and the only arbiter of that happiness: it provides for their security, foresees and supplies their necessities, facilitates their pleasures, manages their principal concerns, directs their industry, regulates the descent of property, and subdivides their inheritances—what remains but to spare them all the care of thinking and all the trouble of living?

Thus it every day renders the exercise of the free agency of man less useful and less frequent; it circumscribes the will within a narrower range, and gradually robs a man of all the uses of himself. The principle of equality has prepared men for these things. It has predisposed them to endure them, and often-times to look upon them as benefits.

This kind of government, idealized as the epitome of beneficence by visionaries of security, is not to be voted into office. It is to be attained indirectly, by means of a strategy called Fabian socialism.

The term "Fabian" relates to the strategy employed by the Roman general Quintus Fabius Maximus against Hannibal in the Second Punic War. Fabius carefully avoided direct and decisive battles, but by unceasing harassment ultimately won his victory. Similarly, the strategy of Fabian socialism is one whereby the central issues are never drawn clearly and presented to the citizens for their unqualified approval or rejection. Harassment is directly against capitalism and competition. All sorts of undesirable effects, from war to criminality, are charged against private enterprise. Accomplishments of the system are either ignored or are credited to other circumstances. At the same time, shining virtues are attributed to cooperation and collectivism and to the social planning programs through which they are to be attained.

Earlier socialists or communists apparently failed to realize that "scientific" social planning is inevitable in the functioning of the type of government they envision. They also failed to realize that the notion of conscious "scientific" social planning would have a tremendous appeal to intellectuals.

John Jewkes, in his *Ordeal by Planning*, contends that the idea of central planning originated in Germany during 1914-1918 as a technique for the more effective administration of the war, but that

... it came to real life when Lenin ... in 1920 wrote this to Krzhizhanovsky: "Couldn't you produce a plan (not a technical but a political scheme) which would be understood by the proletariat? For instance in ten years (or five?) we shall build 20 (or 30 or 50?) power stations." *(P. 2)*

In America, as with other countries affected by Fabian socialism, no overall plan is proposed in forthright fashion for us to accept or reject on its merits. Instead, the planning affects first one segment of our affairs and then another, so that we never do view the process in its total perspective.

My thesis is that the type of social planning which characterizes our society follows a fairly regular pattern. The social planning

(1) begins in a time of crisis, usually a crisis associated either with war or with economic depression;

(2) it starts with a program which relates only to a specific economic situation;

(3) it continues after the crisis has passed and different reasons (excuses) are created to justify its continuance; and

(4) it overflows the confines of the strictly economic area and expands into areas political and social.

The Parity Program

During the first world war, large quantities of food were needed to feed our own Armed Forces and to supply allies. With a large demand for food, prices rose and farmers expanded production. Much sooner than was anticipated, however, European agricultural production was restored after hostilities ceased. European demand for American crops dwindled sharply and suddenly, while farmers continued to produce on the vast wartime scale. Prices for farm products plummeted. Many farmers had expanded their holdings on mortgage. The return for their products diminished to a point where it no longer sufficed to meet mortgage payments. This was the economic crisis which ultimately gave rise to the parity program.

This very real crisis could have been met directly with long-term loans at low rates of interest, or with no interest charge at all. It might even have been met by outright gifts. Instead of meeting the crisis specifically, a plan was devised. The plan was the parity program. Behind this program was the laudable notion that farmers' incomes should be raised to a level comparable with those of factory workers—that "parity" should exist between the two types of incomes. In simplified fashion, the program can be described as a governmental guarantee that farmers would receive payments for their crops which would enable them to maintain the standard of living which they had had in the good years from 1909 to 1914.

The farm crisis of the early 1920s passed. The dormant idea of parity continued its germination.

During the depression of the 1930s it was nurtured by fear into full flower. For reasons less obvious—and ones frequently inconsistent—the idea continued to grow after economic recovery in the late 1930s, during the years of the second world war, and during the prosperous postwar years down to the present. Not only has the program continued, it has expanded to prodigious degree and at almost incalculable cost. And as it has expanded it has encroached upon political areas to restrict the freedom of farmers and others, as will be described.

Social Security

To meet the crises of impoverished old age, and of the destitution associated with widespread unemployment during the economic depression—and as a measure to prevent future depressions —the Social Security Act was passed in 1935. It, too, had laudable goals in that the Government now seemed to assist people to save for a pension in their advanced years and to provide them with an income if they became unemployed through no fault of their own. Further, pensions received by retired workers, and unemployment compensation received by those out of work would, it was contended, bolster the economy. Through an accumulation of reserve funds during prosperous times, economic depression would be prevented.

Since that time Social Security has expanded to huge proportions and gives promise of further expansion in the future. To greater and greater degree it becomes a political issue. It is also a personal issue as it restricts freedom through governmental compulsion.

Many meritorious features are associated with the parity program, with the social security program, and with other legislation which involves social planning. Here I wish only to stress that such governmental ventures are a reflection of the vision that Utopia in the form of economic security can be attained through planning; that we, by degrees and without clear awareness of the course we take, now join the ranks of visionaries in a quest for security, planned and governmentally guaranteed.

[111]

Chapter VII

The Source: Scientism and Fear

CHANGED conditions of living join with changed
beliefs to encourage our acceptance of a vision
of personal emancipation. Life in cities promotes segmentaliza-
tion of personality, with stress on superficial materialistic qualities outweighing consideration of deeper traits of character. Social controls operate less effectively in large cities than in smaller
communities. Such conditions of life conjoin with scientistic theories of human behavior to distend or dissolve social controls. A
situation results wherein more than ever before we need a high
degree of intestinal fortitude to resist temptation. Because it is
less understood than other factors which give rise to the vision
of personal emancipation, the influence of scientism has been
stressed in this development. Such stress on pseudo-scientific
theories which affect our beliefs should not lead us to ignore the
setting in which they operate.

The quest for security through supposedly scientifically planned
programs should also be viewed from a perspective which includes profound changes in economic conditions. These changes
in the economic *milieu* constitute a matrix within which our
changed beliefs take shape. Though an understanding of changed
economic conditions contributes to our comprehension of the
changed beliefs, it by no means follows that the beliefs are a direct and inescapable result of economic determinism.

While it may readily be granted that economic conditions form
a background which highlights our changed beliefs, we should
keep in mind that a variety of social and political factors also

plays a part in the process. We should, too, remember that the ideas which constitute an essential ingredient in the vision of security through scientific planning *preceded* rather than followed the economic conditions which (according to economic determinism) were supposed to create this type of thinking. Further doubt is cast upon the assumptions of economic determinism when we think of countries which reorganized their existence around the planning idea even though the economic conditions which supposedly constitute the source of the ideas had never existed. Russia itself is an illustration of this precedence of ideas over conditions, and control of China by communists is an even more striking example.

As a background, and as an influencing condition rather than a determining cause, some of the changes in the productive process will be outlined before describing the ideological catalyst which already has jelled much of our economic life into the mold of social planning.

The Industrial Revolution

Use of power other than that supplied by men or animals marked the profound change in the production of goods which is generally called the Industrial Revolution. Central to the developments of the Industrial Revolution was the steam engine. Many centuries ago, two hundred years before the birth of Christ, Hero of Alexandria had described an engine which would operate by steam. In 1698 Thomas Savery developed an engine which was of some commercial use, but it was through the improvements of Thomas Newcomen in 1711 and of James Watt in 1769 that steam power began to revolutionize the processes of production.

The textile industry of England was the first economic area to be revolutionized. Inventions which speeded up the weaving of thread into cloth were followed by those which enabled lint to be spun into thread much faster than even the new weaving processes could use it up. Further inventions were needed to speed still more the weaving process. In 1793, power looms were invented. Well might one wonder if necessity is the mother of invention, or if invention is the mother of necessity.

One result of the greatly expanded productive capacity of the British textile industry was a need for more raw material to supply the machines. Much of this raw material was cotton, grown in America. Amounts of cotton which could be fed to the expanding British textile factories were limited because of the laborious and time-consuming process involved in separating the seeds from the lint. This problem was solved in 1792 by Eli Whitney's invention of the cotton gin. Cotton growers could now expand their acreage. With expanded acreage arose the need for more workers to plant, care for and pick the crop. Slavery filled this need, and slavery expanded rapidly. One might allow his imagination to roam, and carry on the chain of circumstances thus: Expanded slavery gave rise to abolitionist sentiments in the North. During the Civil War a Republican was President of the United States. Therefore, the reason the majority of Southerners vote Democratic today is because Thomas Newcomen improved the steam engine in 1711!

The links in this series of circumstances are made to illustrate how easy it is to develop plausible but over-simplified theories. Obviously, many political and social factors were involved.

Substitution of steam power for human and animal power enabled factories to spring up, and increased the production of goods, but however important the increase in factories was to our economy, another revolution in productive processes was needed to bring into being our modern economic conditions. It is not merely a factory system which constitutes the most distinctive element in our methods of production; rather, it is the introduction of the mass-production system into the factories.

Mass-Production

Many factors were involved in developing the mass-production system which so uniquely characterizes the American economy. Standardized and interchangeable parts are one of these necessary elements.

In 1798, the same Eli Whitney who had invented the cotton gin was awarded a contract by Congress to make several thousand rifles for the Army. Long months passed, and the legislators became convinced that they were being cheated by a crack-pot when Whitney failed to produce a single one. Up until that time, rifles had been tailor-made by gunsmiths. One man might work faster than another, or with greater skill, but each separately fashioned individual guns. Eli Whitney devised a new technique. For the first time, or at least for the first time on a large scale, specifications were drawn up so that parts could be produced separately, with each part fitting into the others. Instead of highly skilled gunsmiths individually fashioning complete rifles, workers less skilled could make parts which were separate and standardized.

Another vital ingredient in the mass-production system is an assembly line to allow workers to remain in one place while their work is conveyed to them. Several industries had adopted assembly-line procedures in their manufacturing process but Henry

Ford was the first to develop its full potentialities in dramatic fashion. As described in *The Big Change*, by Frederick Lewis Allen,

> .... In 1913 he put in his first assembly-line, and by the beginning of 1914 he was producing the entire car on the assembly-line principle. Each workman performed a single operation; each element of the car went on a power-driven moving conveyor platform past a series of these workmen, each of whom added or fixed in place some part of it; and these various assembly lines converged upon a main conveyor platform on which the chassis moved to completion. *(P. 111)*

These principles soon spread to produce goods in unprecedented quantities and to create the wealthiest society ever known to man.

In addition to assembly lines and standardized, interchangeable parts, other characteristics are inescapably associated with this highly successful productive technique. Most of these features have implications that are social and political as well as economic. Mass-production requires a high degree of division of labor in which individual workers contribute only a small fraction of the complete product. Workers make parts of things, instead of things. And here they suffer a psychological loss; they are deprived of the sense of satisfaction associated with creativity. For associated with mass-production is the process of decreasing the amount of training necessary to perform a job. Jobs are "de-skilled", simplified so that they entail no more than a few motions, easily-learned. The more complicated tasks are performed by ever more perfected machines. In a way at least, workers as well as parts become standardized and interchangeable.

Several conditions are associated with the relationship between mass-production and large units of production. By its nature, mass-production is economical only if performed on a large scale. Many workers were needed in one area and thus large factories stimulated the growth of large cities. With improvements in power supply and in transportation, the need to locate large factories in or near large cities becomes less imperative, and factories can be more widely distributed. Efficiency resulting from a high degree of mechanization requires expensive machinery and this, in turn, demands a large investment of capital. Huge capital requirements compelled the development of corporations, with thousands of investors contributing their money through the purchase of stock. Relationships between workers and employers lost their personal touch due not only to the magnitude of productive enterprises but also to the characteristics of corporate operation. Many of the stockholders had little or no knowledge of the physical plant or of the personnel of the corporations in which they invested their money. With the necessity for huge investments the number of capitalists who personally owned and operated large productive units, decreased. Professional managers were employed to perform specialized functions relating to production, finance, personnel relations, etc. So pronounced has been this trend that there is some merit for the contention that ours is more nearly a managerial economy than it is a capitalistic one. While the essentials of capitalism remain in the form of competition and private enterprise, single owner-controllers of large businesses are being replaced by teams of managers, each a specialist in his field. In the sense that these managers can change from one corporation to another and perform equally well, they also, like the workers and like the parts of the product, are interchangeable.

As productive work became simplified and gradually required less physical strength, women were able to find employment as factory operatives. With the problems of production solved by increased use of machinery, problems of distribution required the services of larger numbers. Percentagewise, white-collar workers increased more than factory operatives. Instead of workers being ground down into dire poverty (as Marx had predicted); instead of machines producing ever-higher profits by displacing workers; wages and employment rose markedly as compared with the costs of the articles of mass-production.

Henry Ford was so farsighted as to dramatize this feature of our economy which still continues to confound the socialists. He completed his first assembly-line in 1914. Thereupon, instead of accumulating huge profits by maintaining the same prices and paying the same rates of wages, Ford did two things: He not only reduced prices but startled the entire industrial world by voluntarily raising wages from the average of $2.40 for a nine-hour day to a minimum of $5.00 for an eight-hour day. (Though $5.00 per day seems a small wage now, let us remember that $5.00 then was the equivalent of approximately $20.00 today.)

Thus, sometimes voluntarily, at other times through pressures exerted by competition, prices are kept at reasonable level. Sometimes voluntarily, at other times through pressures exerted by unions which now counterbalance the influence of owners and managers, wages have been raised to provide mass purchasing power for the products of the mass-production system.

Another vital aspect of the system needs to be mentioned, and that is the high degree of interdependence involved in its functioning. On a simple level, it is not difficult for a worker to understand that a breakdown of one section of an assembly-line can shut down the entire process, or that a strike involving a few key workers can make thousands unemployed. It is more difficult to comprehend how a strike of electrical workers in Pittsburgh requires wholesale lay-offs among automobile workers in Detroit, or how an inter-union disagreement in the coal mines of West Virginia causes steel plants in Pennsylvania to close down. An intricate interrelationship between a wide variety of raw materials, power, and products is necessarily associated with mass-production.

The complexities of this interrelationship, coupled with the loss of personal relations between employees and employers, promotes in the worker a feeling that he is at the mercy of forces which he cannot comprehend, and sponsor in him a desire to find some agency—his union, or the Government, or both—which will protect his livelihood from influences which to him are incomprehensible but vital.

These vague presentiments of impersonal and incomprehensible economic forces crystallized during the economic depression of the 1930s. Though for some time flaws had been evident in the economic structure, a false and hectic delusion of continuous and unprecedented prosperity prevailed in 1929. In a summary twenty-four years later, *The New York Times* recounted the advice of the Democratic national chairman, John J. Raskob:

> If a man saves $15 a week and invests in good common stocks and allows the dividends and rights to accumulate, at the end of twenty years he will have . . . an income from investments of around $400 a month. He will be rich. And because income can do that, I am firm in my belief that any one not only can be rich but ought to be rich.

Similar visions of a "new economic era" were espoused by numerous economists right down to the very day—October 29, 1929—which still is known as "Black Tuesday". Stocks whose quotations averaged $312 a short ten days previously were down to $200 a share by the end of trading. On that day investors and speculators lost $8,000,000,000 of their paper profits.

The Great Depression

The stock market crash of October 29, 1929 signalized the beginning of a long and serious economic depression. In addition to billions of dollars lost by people who had invested in the market, millions of other people saw their savings vanish as banks and Building and Loan agencies failed. Prices of farm commodities dropped so low that, in many cases, it was more economical to let them rot than to incur the expense of harvesting and marketing them. With savings wiped out, the market for factory products declined, and despite reductions in prices and drastic wage-cuts many factories and stores had to cease business. Unemployment mounted on a nationwide scale to produce a hardship which hit tragically millions of American families.

Economists sometimes attempt to explain economic depression by attributing it to an excess of productive capacity over effective consumer demand. Such interpretations describe a condition which exists during a depression; they do not explain what factors cause the condition to occur. Even now, with the benefit of hindsight, no scientifically accurate theory of the causes of economic depression has been developed. Economic predictions prior to 1929 not only failed to indicate what was about to happen, but in many instances indicated the very opposite. In the years since that time the record of scientific prediction has been no better. When disastrous depression spread during the 1930s, no one really knew why it happened. No one knew how serious it would be, how long it would last, or what measures would produce recovery—then or now.

With uncertainty clouding the causes while poverty spread through the Land, prodigious efforts were made to alleviate conditions. Measures taken early during the depression were primarily of a financial nature. The Federal Government provided assistance only indirectly. The measures included grants to States, loans to business, and programs of public works.

Then, soon after Franklin D. Roosevelt assumed the Presidency in 1933, the Federal Government embarked upon a series of projects in an attempt to cope with the problem directly and on a national basis. The Federal Emergency Relief Administration (FERA) continued with grants to States for direct relief, but gradually concentrated its activities on work relief, at first under the Civil Works Administration (CWA), later (in 1935) through the Works Projects Administration (WPA). State and local governments contributed no more than nominal sums to such programs and the Federal Government assumed primary responsibility to relieve economic conditions. Much debate centered around the participation of the Federal Government as a virtual employer of millions of citizens. Some contended that such action was necessary to prevent calamitous destitution, others argued that such make-work projects sapped the independence of citizens and created a politically potent device through which an administration could perpetuate its power.

The National Industrial Recovery Act (NRA) attempted to stimulate economic conditions through voluntary agreements between businesses to keep both wages and prices from falling. This Act was declared unconstitutional. The National Youth Authority (NYA) helped students to continue their education by working at jobs made possible through grants of Federal assistance. For young people who were out of school and out of work the Civilian Conservation Corps (CCC) combined work-relief with conservation projects. Whatever the indirect effects of these measures, they did serve to alleviate some of the immediate distress.

Our concern in this analysis, however, is with the measures which evolved out of the depression and which were designed as continuing programs, not merely as stop-gaps. Let us first look into the ideas which, long existing but dormant, emerged into programs under the stress of fear and uncertainty which prevailed during the depression years.

Intellectuals, and the Source

Through the years leading up to the Great Depression students and the public alike had been subjected to many highly critical and one-sided interpretations of capitalism by historians and other intellectuals. A summary of such portrayal of our economic development appears in F. A. Hayek's *Capitalism and the Historians*. Describing this critical interpretation as it occurred in England, T. S. Ashton, one of the contributors to Hayek's book, tells how the phrase "Industrial Revolution" was employed by prominent historians (and previously by Marx and Engels) to persuade students that the introduction of large-scale production was a social catastrophe rather than the miraculous fulfillment of man's material needs which it was.

Poor working conditions in mines and factories were luridly described, and the exploitation of child workers became a focal point for humanitarian sympathy. As in all effective propaganda, some basis did exist for these descriptions. Working conditions in mines and factories were undesirable—but so were working conditions on farms. Children did work in mines and factories, but children had always been put to work as soon as they were physically able. As factories developed, children, instead of working for nothing, began to work for pay.

Though seriously undesirable conditions were attendant upon the development of industrial capitalism, most of these and similar hardships had prevailed long before. Graphic descriptions which depicted excessive hardships as arising solely out of the system failed to mention the benefits of increased production, and on the other hand attributed the social advances to governmental legislation which improved working conditions. Many pupils, here as well as in England, thus received first and enduring impressions that from its very inception capitalism's chief products were hardship and suffering; that deprivation and sorrow were originated and fostered by capitalism, while all economic progress welled from boundlessly beneficent governments.

Of course there were shortsighted and selfish employers who took advantage of their employees; there also were considerate ones who pioneered in improvements. We tend to forget that government is essentially non-productive, that our economic and social gains can be *directed* by legislation but that their origin, and the sole source of their continuance, exists in increased production made possible by the efficiency in the economic system.

In recent years prominent historians have admitted that in the past, commonly if not characteristically, members of their profession have presented a biased view of business in their textbooks and in their teaching. One reaction to the frank acknowledgement of a former bias (and much of it still prevails) would be to applaud the social scientists who see and admit the distortions which colored earlier interpretations. But such admissions also lend credence to George Orwell's contention that society can be changed by re-writing history so that it supports a particular prejudice or design. We must not forget that the textbooks which were so scathingly critical of business were not read and accepted as the interpretation of any one man, but as proved fact based on unimpeachable data processed by an unquestionably accurate method. If, as is now at times admitted, bias was presented as validated social science in the recent past, how can we be sure of its objectivity in the future?

Some of the ways in which intellectuals fostered hostile attitudes toward capitalism and contemptuous distrust of businessmen are described in Edward N. Saveth's "What Historians Teach about Business". In the earlier part of the century, writers such as Lincoln Steffens and Ida Tarbell proudly wore the designation "muckraker" as their books and articles drew a picture of cynically irresponsible businessmen whose unquenchable greed was only partially sated by mountainous profits. As cited by Mr. Saveth, Lincoln Steffens, driven to self-stirred desperation by his own horrific caricature of business evils, sent this appeal for succor to the American Communist Party:

> Communism can solve our problem. . . . That is my muckraker's proclamation; that the American Communist party program meets our American capitalist situation precisely, and it is the only American party that meets it—head on. . . .

No matter how vehemently hostile their attacks upon private business, no matter how widely circulated their writings, the diatribes of "muckrakers" could still be rejected by most, and their acceptance limited to those whose disgruntlement with the system made their persuasion easy. The muckrakers, though colorful, were less influential in creating the vision than were others. Aided by the prestige of authoritarianism and of science, skilled in the arts of subtle persuasion, academic intellectuals were more influential by far. They convinced their captive *student* audiences of the evils of business and of the vast beneficence of government.

Highly influential on the receptive minds of many professors of history, economics and sociology was Charles A. Beard's *An Economic Interpretation of the Constitution* (1913). Professor Beard's book contained favorable observations about our economic system and sympathetic comments about representative business men, but it did stress the role of economic influences on our early history. In his later years Beard acknowledged that the views in his book resulted from the necessary distortion involved in any examination of a complicated topic from one single angle. Despite his protests, many influential professors based their own writings and lectures on his book as definitive proof that the Constitution of the United States was devised primarily to protect and enhance the interests of business. Prominent among more recent works of historians who attempt to convince students that "the businessman was the villain of the past as well as of the present" is Vernon L. Parrington's *Main Currents in American Thought,* and *The Age of Jackson,* by Arthur M. Schlesinger, Jr. These more recent works take the next step in creating the vision as they portray "liberals" (in the sense of advocates of governmental regulation or control of business) as intrepid heroes who rescue us from the havoc wrought by villainous businessmen.

To create a vision of planned security through governmental control, you first formulate a background. This is done in two ways: Openly, by diatribes; and, more subtly, by slanted interpretations which smear the accomplishments of private enterprise. Against this background, untested promises for the future gleam radiantly in contrast.

This technique of creating the vision was, and still is, commonly employed. The works cited constitute merely a few of the more influential ones from which scores of others emerged. In an earlier book I analyzed almost a hundred sociology textbooks to determine the nature and extent of such influence. In *The Claims of Sociology,* specific illustrations show the manner in which many authors of sociology textbooks create the vision by portraying the glowing promises of benefits to be derived from social planning and collectivism against the dark background of private enterprise which they have painted. This raises the following question about the educational ethics of such techniques:

Authors of sociology texts offer little more than glittering and seductive generalities as alternatives which are presented

[121]

in gleaming contrast to their gloomy forebodings and criticisms of existing economic conditions. Is a presentation which criticizes a functioning system by contrasting it with hypothetical remedies which are believed to be attainable in nonexistent alternative systems justified in textbooks which are presented to immature and receptive minds under the authoritarian prestige of science?   *(P. 81)*

Additional indication of the persistence with which intellectuals engage in extreme criticism of capitalism is contained in J. A. Schumpeter's *Capitalism, Socialism, and Democracy.* Abundant evidence of the intellectuals' penchant for planning can be found in scores of textbooks and in articles in "scientific" journals by the hundreds. The theme is a contrast between a dingy, besmirched capitalism and the gleaming mirage of a planned society. Thus the vision emerges.

Many of us have supposed that radical political movements such as socialism and communism result from protest or revolt by simple farmers or laborers. This belief is one which socialists, and particularly communists, foster. Actually, the *leaders* in both of these movements, in America as well as in Russia and other countries, always have been and still are primarily from the middle and upper classes. Most of those who are drawn toward such movements are not recruited from the ranks of workers, but from the ranks of the intellectuals—the authors, professors, clergymen, actors, and from the men and women of the scientific and social world. Few have realized the powerful influence which professional men and women—intellectuals—exert to divorce society from its traditions and to beguile others to pursue the vision.

Intellectuals, and the Communist Vision

In his analysis of the background of the Bolshevik revolution, titled *Stalin,* Nikolaus Basseches recounts that Lenin (the intellectual leader of the revolution) was the son of His Excellency Counsellor of State Ulyanov, and proceeds to list the middle or upper class origins of virtually all of the other leaders of the communist revolution. Salvadori, in *The Rise of Modern Communism,* emphasizes the major role played by intellectuals, and after referring to documentary sources on the Bolshevik revolution, concludes:

> This would seem to support the opinion of those who maintain that communism is not so much a "proletarian" movement as an expression of extreme dissatisfaction among the intellectual section of the middle classes.
>
> *(Footnote, p. 20)*

In their *Report on the American Communist* for which they interviewed and examined the histories of almost 300 former communists, M. L. Ernst and D. Loth note that "Most of the Communists occupy positions which do not call for any work with their hands. They seem to be found more often in the professions which are entirely intellectual or in jobs which call for no manual dexterity." Perhaps this reaffirms the wisdom of the adage that the devil finds work for idle hands to do!

As for the futility of the notion that communism results from ignorance and can be successfully combated by education,

> The average Communist has had far more schooling than the general population of the country, and the proportion of party members who have been to college is very high. Even more striking is the great number of graduate degrees among them. *(Pp. 3-4)*

Should skeptical readers still question the appeal which movements such as communism and socialism have for intellectuals, here is a statement from one who speaks with unquestionable authority. The leader of the teachers section of the Communist Party, J. Mason, addressed the tenth convention of the Party (New York State, 1938) as follows:

> There are several hundred party members in the union. This is a big fraction and more than is necessary in our industry, if you wish to call it that. I think about 100 or so would be sufficient to work within the union; and so we have sent our Party members into the apparatus of our Party everywhere, in the counties, in the sections, and in the districts. You fall over teachers everywhere. . . .

It might be worthwhile to mull over the significance of this boast. Is it not just a bit ironical that teachers who were communists were ordered by the Party to infiltrate other occupations so that they, the teacher-intellectuals, could persuade actual workers that workers were being exploited and oppressed?

Most teachers were not, and are not, communists. But never forget that communism does not need, and does not seek, a majority. The movement requires only a small percentage of actual party members. These few purposeful individuals can dominate and manipulate the larger groups. Teachers Union Local No. 5, for example, with a few members exerted vital influence over thousands of teachers in the New York area. Burn into your brain the fact that a few dedicated persons can dominate many times their own numerical strength. This is the essence of the technique of infiltration and control.

As an illustration of the appeal of communism among another professional group, the 1951 annual report of the House Committee on Un-American Activities concluded that Committee's study of Communist Party membership in the motion picture industry by declaring:

It must be stated that if the same number of Communists existed in every segment of American life as in the case of Hollywood motion-picture writers during past years, the United States would be in a precarious position.   (P. 8)

Fellow-Travelers, and the Vision

Much more effective in spreading the vision than those who openly admit their Party membership or who clearly avow their intent are those who conceal their sympathies under a mask of guileless objectivity; those who shelter them beneath the protecting cloak of science; those who parade them under the banner of "progress" or the halo of humanitarianism.

Many of these (conscious or unwitting) sympathizers now actively repudiate Soviet communism; some because the practices associated with it violate their humanitarian sentiments, others because, as Whittaker Chambers expressed it, "They lack the character for Communist faith because they lack the character for any faith." Those who would change the world according to their intellectual schemes but who lack sufficient strength of conviction to adhere to the party which most nearly incorporates their ideas in its practice, Chambers describes as spiritual vagrants "whose traditional faith has been leached out in the bland climate of rationalism."

Communists are acutely aware that open identification with their movement destroys the value of the influence exerted by intellectuals. Such people are valued more for the indirect aid derived from their sympathies than for any party membership. A former member of the Communist Party described this strategy to the House Committee on Un-American Activities:

Our program must be to gain our ends through our friends, sympathizers, and allies while keeping ourselves in the background. As Soviet power grows there will be a greater aversion to Communist Parties everywhere. So we must practice the techniques of withdrawal—never appear in the foreground—let our friends do our work. We must always remember that one sympathizer is worth generally more than a dozen militant Communists. A university professor who, without being a party member, lends himself to the interest of the Soviet Union is worth more than a hundred men with party cards.

In their detailed analysis of *Socialism and American Life*, Egbert and Persons emphasize the importance of this indirect influence. They describe how fellow-travelers shaped opinion in the late 1930s through their positions in publishing houses, on magazines, in Hollywood and on the radio. Later, the communist intellectual influence spread to include not only sympathetic assistance from those engaged in literary and artistic professions but important support from other intellectual groups as well:

> ... The wheel turned and picked up the college professors, the ministers, and lastly the scientists. In the later years the proportion of ministers among the sucker lists of communist fronts was probably higher than any other group. Bewitched by the communist myth, unable to believe evil, attracted by the opportunity to do good, the ministers moved blissfully about, unaware of the shadowy figures behind them. In the latter half of the forties, scientists for the first time began appearing in greater number on communist "innocent" or fellow-traveling fronts, attracted, apparently, not by the utopian and Christian elements in the communist appeal, but by its tough-mindedness and power role. . . .   *(Vol. 1, p. 365)*

Though a primary source of the vision can be traced to the influence of intellectuals whose portrayal of planned security glowed in bright contrast to their gloomy forebodings about competitive enterprise, many conditions associated with mass-production also contributed to our quest for security through governmental planning. In the following chapters some fallacies and hazards associated with our excursion into the wonderland of governmental planning will be described, but though I emphasize the delusion and the confusion it should be remembered that many desirable qualities also are associated with such efforts.

Yet the challenge cannot be met simply by identifying its source. If the source were openly identical with the international conspiracy of communism it could be controlled by the F.B.I. If it were admittedly a program of the Socialist Party it could be accepted or rejected by votes. Most of those who promote the vision are members of neither party. They are motivated by humanitarianism, and are firmly convinced by a secular materialistic rationality. The essence of today's challenge lies precisely in the fact that it is not clear-cut, that it involves much more than an ability to distinguish black from white. A dogmatic rejection of all changes which seem to involve some relation to socialism or communism could most seriously handicap our future. We may be equally endangered if the narrow perspective of our separate interests obscures a wider view. This view shows us a combination, which is pulling us along the road to governmental regulation, *i.e.,* to statism.

To insulate ourselves from the intellectual source would extinguish the vision, but it also would plunge us into darkness.

The challenge lies in shading its incandescence so that it does not blind us to reality. We must remember that though brilliance sparks from the sometimes crossed wires of the intellect, light's source is from the timeless realistic sun, its reflection from the romantic moon, its consecration from translucent windows of worship.

The Source: Scientism, and Fear

In the serious depression of the 1930s the impersonal nature of the mass-production system combined with an ignorance of its complex interrelationships to produce uncertainty, and fear. Widespread unemployment, low prices, foreclosures, and serious economic deprivation created a sense of hopeless desperation. Many economists and other intellectuals (long critical of all real, and numerous imagined, defects in the system of private enterprise) were quick to aggravate the already serious situation. They proclaimed a collapse of fundamental elements of the economic system and decreed a permanently large percentage of unemployment. They pronounced that our productive facilities exceeded our capacity to consume its products; that our industrial equipment was overexpanded and that it should be reduced. Such were the "scientific predictions of the experts".

Fortunately for us we had no time to put this "scientific" advice into practice. Before we could reduce our industrial plant we were engaged in frantic efforts to expand it. Within a few years the dire forebodings of large bodies of unemployed were replaced by the actuality of a shortage of workers. Our professional crystal-gazers failed to foresee these events.

Thousands of us in our student years had listened to the glowing promises of scientific economic planning. Many others had read such ideas. Few paid them any more attention than they were worth—until the depression.

Uncertainty—and the desperate fear of economic hardship—then drained the oxygen from the economic atmosphere and created a vacuum into which the ideas of scientific planning would pour. Mistaking for cancer its painful cramps, the ailing society swallowed strange nostrums.

Many expedient measures were taken to offset the grievous effects of economic depression. For the most part these were confined to direct efforts to cope with specific situations. Various relief measures were of this sort, claiming nothing more than to attempt to alleviate specific symptoms. In this category were loans to business firms. Less direct, and more complicated in their implications—but still essentially temporary expedients—were the Works Projects Administration, Civilian Conservation Corps and National Youth Administration. Though such measures involved an intervention by the Federal Government vastly greater than ever before, they were looked upon as temporary incursions, to be withdrawn when no longer needed. Other measures, however, incorporated elements of permanency and planning.

One of the many factors involved in our acceptance of these programs of permanent "scientific" planning was a marked change in our beliefs about the causes of poverty and the responsibility for it. Though the significant origin of this change occurred fifty years before, a half-century is a comparatively short time in historical perspective. It was not until the late 1930s that changed beliefs in regard to poverty gained general acceptance. They were then to exert a profound influence upon economics, upon politics, and upon individual behavior.

Back in 1905 poverty-stricken people were divided into two categories: the worthy and the unworthy. Worthy poor people included widows, orphans, and the physically handicapped. They were looked upon as deserving of charity. Drunkards, the sinful, and those who were lazy or improvident, were helped only to protect society from their contagion. Poverty was considered to be a matter of individual responsibility. Then, in 1905, the British Poor Law Commission submitted a report. Though this report reaffirmed the beliefs which generally prevailed about the nature of poverty, two members filed a minority report which presented an opposite view. In this minority report, Beatrice and Sidney Webb, who were among the founders of the Fabian socialist movement in England, contended that the burden of responsibility for poverty rested not with individuals but upon society.

It was this minority report which came to be taught and emphasized by economists and sociologists.

The Webbs soon afterward (1911) published *The Prevention of Destitution,* in which they outlined their Fabian strategy (though not identifying it as such) by which poverty would be "cured". Their program included socialized medicine, minimum wages, and public spending to relieve cyclical economic depressions. Others wrote along the same lines, and even before the depression struck us in the 1930s, many scholars and students were ready to accept the notion that individuals have no responsibility for their poverty; that society, which causes it, is obligated to eliminate it. Coupled with this belief was the popularization of a doctrine that the government could prevent depressions by building up financial reserves during prosperity and spending such reserves to prevent a serious economic decline.

Fear and confusion associated with the depression of the thirties opened the doors to let part of the vision shine through. In addition to expedient measures aimed at limited alleviation of temporary conditions, we embarked on planning programs. Included in this category were such enactments as the Agricultural Adjustment Administration (1933), the Social Security Act (1935), and the Fair Labor Standards Act (1938). These differed from direct and limited efforts to cope with specific problems arising out of the depression in that they were based on supposedly scientific doctrines; in that they were indirect; and in that they were designed to regulate permanently important aspects of the economy.

The Agricultural Adjustment Administration was proposed by Professor Milburn L. Wilson and sponsored by another former academician, Rexford Guy Tugwell. It envisioned governmental regulation of prices for farm commodities through crop curtailment (by governmental subsidies in the form of rentals to take acreage out of production). Together with the establishment of the Commodity Credit Corporation (1933) to provide crop loans on excess production, it constituted a tremendous elaboration of the parity program set up years before. Minimum wages and maximum hours were fixed by the Fair Labor Standards Act to spread the work and to act as a cushion against depressions in the future.

Unemployment Compensation and Old Age and Survivors Insurance were the planning features of the Social Security Act. Both were indirect and permanent and both were based on "scientific" proof that reserve funds built up during prosperity would act as a firm brake whenever the economy threatened to slide into depression.

Much direct humanitarian good has been accomplished by these programs which now implement the vision. They are all extremely popular, so popular that they virtually are political "sacred cows". People are so pleased with them that it seems almost indecent even to raise questions about them. Yet, despite their desirable features, they possess serious defects which only belatedly and only in part are being revealed to the public. Further, inherent in them are implications which have been almost totally ignored.

The reality of these implications as they relate to the Fair Labor Standards Act and to the Social Security Act will be described in the next chapter, and discussed in relation to the parity program. That program will be cited in some detail as an object lesson in the hazards of social planning.

Chapter VIII

The Reality: (*a*) Public Delusion

S OME are tempted to exaggerate the political situation in America with impassioned warnings that we have already stumbled into the gutter of socialism and now lie prostrate under the heels of planners and social engineers. True, we have incorporated into our social organization and into our economic system many elements of socialist programs. Those socialist proposals which we have adopted, however, have been geared into the machinery of what is still essentially a private enterprise economy.

On the other hand, at least equally in error are those who scoff at the influence of socialistic planners and who minimize the significance of changes which they have sponsored.

Nurtured by fear and uncertainty during the 1930s, social planning ideas—which previously grew only in the soil and climate of an intellectual environment—sprang up to wind their stretching tendrils around some of the sturdy branches of the society. They have not choked the roots nor yet destroyed the fruits, but their tinted leaves do intermingle among the verdant growth of the tree of our life—to reflect a different hue.

To show how these vines of social planning have thrust themselves into our national affairs and how they now entangle our lives with their growing profusion, several depression-sponsored programs which incorporate elements of the vision of planned security will be described. No attempt will be made to recount these programs in detail. The characteristics which embody the elements of permanent planning will, however, be outlined. This chapter contains such an outline of the Fair Labor Standards Act and of the Social Security Act. The next chapter centers around the parity program for agricultural commodities. This present chapter will stress the nature of the delusion growing out of our vision of security; the chapter following will emphasize the degree of confusion arising from "scientific" planning.

Before entering into descriptions of these programs, and before portraying the delusion and confusion associated with them, it is advisable to give at least brief mention to the general importance of perspective and to its particular relation to the viewpoint of this analysis.

Perspective Shapes the View

A crawling baby sees his doll-house as a monstrous structure; a pilot looks down upon the checkerboard earth and miniature houses. Burning sun and long dry days bring glee to vacationers; they bring anguish to drought-struck farmers. Ice cream is ambrosia to children, dread poison to a diabetic. Rural folk long for the thrill of a city; urban cave-dwellers yearn for the peace and quiet of a farm. Parents see the "senseless" frivolity of their offspring; youngsters, the stodgy dullness of their elders. Obscured to others is the unalloyed virtue and flawless beauty which lovers see in each other; and it is well known that to them the moon is larger. Drunks are not sure just what they do see; they are certain only that it is double.

Perspective is not alone to shape the contours of what we see, and to tint the view. Our senses are affected by perspective, but they are governed by reality. It is our beliefs which more often are affected by reality, but governed by perspective.

Soon learns a child that the eagerness of his grasp does not imprison the shining star—and then the stars are forever a little dimmed. As giant daddy shrinks to walk the earth with other men—and stumble, too—the child grows, and dreams diminish. Wrinkles, greyness, and bulging hips erase the tracery of young love's gentle etching—and rub away some lines of life's design. Reality's harsh abrasion dims each one's promise to himself. But in our social views we can insulate some of our beliefs from several aspects of reality, and view them from one perspective to the virtual exclusion of others.

An unemployed worker who receives compensation from the Government is likely to view such assistance from an *individual* perspective. He is not likely to be concerned about the broad economic, political or social implications of a Social Security Act. He, or the retired worker who receives a pension, is likely to limit his appraisal to personal gratitude. A great many people, whether direct recipients or not, have been influenced in their evaluation of this Act by an *humanitarian* perspective. Their judgment is influenced, and properly so, by knowledge that many deserving people have obtained sorely needed help from this legislation. Powerful influence exerted by the individual perspective and by the humanitarian perspective makes it hazardous from a *political* perspective to adversely question its operation.

From an *economic* perspective one's view could center on the direct costs of its functioning; upon economic abuses associated with its operation; or, from this perspective, one could analyze the nature of the reserve funds which are being raised for future contingency. From a *societal* perspective one could attempt to assess its overall and long-term influence upon the fabric of the society.

Conclusions which we may hold about legislation such as the Fair Labor Standards Act or the Social Security Act depend very largely upon the perspective from which we view them. From an individual or an humanitarian perspective, they shine in a highly favorable light. Politically, they are virtually untouchable—they seem to help so many so much, and to hurt so few so little. The merits of such legislation are so many and so obvious from these perspectives that they are too well-known to need repeating.

Ceilings and Floors

The Fair Labor Standards Act which was passed in 1938 is frequently referred to as the "Wages and Hours Act" because its main provisions were described as an effort to "put a ceiling over hours and a floor under wages." Maximum hours of work permitted without payment of time-and-a-half for overtime were set at forty-four for the first year after passage of the Act, to be reduced to forty within a few years. Twenty-five cents per hour was established as the minimum wage, to be increased over a period of seven years to forty cents.

In these days it doesn't seem possible that special legislation was required to guarantee an hourly wage of twenty-five cents, but undoubtedly the wages of thousands of workers increased as a result of the Act's provisions. As to the broad economic influence which it was supposed to exert through increased purchasing power and decreased unemployment, there is no sure way to measure. At the time of its passage economic conditions had already markedly improved, and soon afterward expenditures for military purposes further stimulated wages and expanded employment. With its direct effects uncertain, the discussion will center upon some of its implications.

Wage-rates of forty cents per hour were soon made unrealistic, even as minimum levels, by changed economic conditions. In 1949 the minimum was raised to seventy-five cents, and in 1955 to $1.00. This necessity to more than double the minimum wage illustrates a fallacy in attempts to fix such rates by legislative fiat. With the minimum at $1.00, a change in economic conditions might compel employers to lay off men whom they could not afford to pay. They could not lower the hourly rate and keep their men employed; it would be against the law. Thus, at least in theory, attempts to increase purchasing power and to spread employment could actually operate to reduce purchasing power and to aggravate unemployment. Since specific and arbitrary minimums are made unrealistic by changing the economic conditions, an alternative would be to base the minimums on purchasing power. In times of inflation, however, minimum wage adjustments might contribute further to the inflationary spiral, while during economic declines they could contribute to further decline. From an overall economic perspective, therefore, the effects of the Fair Labor Standards Act are of questionable value. Broader in scope are some of the *implications* of this type of legislation.

Congress is given no power by the Constitution to fix minimum wages or to determine the hours of work. To enact such a measure, therefore, the constitutional limitations had to be circumvented. The basis was found in the power which Congress has to regulate interstate commerce.

Constitutional justification for the Act was based upon an allegation that low wages and long hours of work burdened commerce, resulted in unfair competition, and led to labor disputes which, in turn, interfered with the free and orderly flow of goods in interstate commerce. There may be some degree of association between the conditions described and wage scales or hours of work, but an element of duplicity certainly was involved in basing regulation of wages and hours on Congress' power to regulate interstate commerce.

One view of such evasion of constitutional limitations would be to contend that the humanitarian end warranted the means, even if the legislative means themselves were questionable. Another perspective would highlight the ethical breach involved in compromising fundamental principles, even for desirable ends. This temptation is a persistent one, and each successive time we succumb to it with less resistance. There is no way to balance our immediate material gains against intangible long-term losses as increasingly we compromise ancient principles in present practice. But we should remember that for us to accept the expediency that ends justify the means is to forsake our moral right to object when others employ it for far different ends. If we find our warrant in humanitarianism or in short-term economic stress, we break a trail for others to follow as they pursue their individual desires or their own economic gains.

This possibility was stressed in a decision of the Supreme Court (*Adkins v. Children's Hospital* 261 U.S. 525, 1923) wherein a 1918 Act of Congress which fixed minimum wages for women was declared unconstitutional. Justice Sutherland trenchantly summed up the disquieting implications of such legislation, and the reasoning then is valid now:

> Finally, it may be said that if, in the interest of the public welfare, the police power may be invoked to justify the fixing of a minimum wage, it may, when the public welfare is thought to require it, be invoked to justify a maximum wage. The power to fix high wages connotes, by like reasoning, the power to fix low wages. If, in the face of the guaranties of the 5th Amendment, this form of legislation shall be legally justified, the field for the operation of the police power will have been widened to a great and dangerous degree. If, for example, in the opinion of future lawmakers, wages in the building trades shall become so high as to preclude people of ordinary means from building and owning homes, an authority which sustains the minimum wage will be invoked to support a maximum wage for building laborers and artisans, and the same argument which has been here urged to strip the employer of his constitutional liberty of contract in one direction will be utilized to strip the employee of his constitutional liberty of contract in the opposite direction. A wrong decision does not end with itself; it is a precedent, and, with the swing of sentiment, its bad influence may run from one extremity of the arc to the other.

In citing the possibility that maximum wages in the building industry might be fixed by law to enable people to afford adequate housing, Mr. Justice Sutherland pointedly illustrated how one humanitarian goal can conflict with another. As we accept expediency as a warrant to attain humanitarian ends we should appreciate that such ends can conflict with each other as well as with personal, economic, or societal goals. To thus accept expediency involves not only a weakening of moral fiber, not only the sacrifice of some known features of society for others unknown, but a risk that the very ends most ardently sought at the moment will themselves at some future turn of events be sacrificed—to expediency.

It should not be inferred from this analysis that legislation such as the Fair Labor Standards Act is bad, nor that those who sponsor it are evil in contrast to those who oppose it. The situation is not so simple as to fit neatly into such clear-cut categories. My stress upon adverse implications associated with this Act, and with the Social Security Act, is to balance an appreciation for their clearly desirable effects with an awareness of influences which are intangible, and frequently undesirable and overlooked.

Socially Secure

The preamble of the Social Security Act of 1935 describes its purpose as

> An Act to provide for the general welfare by establishing a system of Federal old-age benefits, and by enabling the several States to make more adequate provision for aged persons, blind persons, dependent and crippled children, maternal and child welfare, public health, and the administration of their unemployment compensation laws; to establish a Social Security Board; to raise revenue; and for other purposes.

The Act contains ten "titles", or principal sections. These may be coupled under three main topics: Public Assistance, Unemployment Compensation, and Old Age and Survivors Insurance. Since the philosophy and practices associated with the public assistance features of the Act constitute fewer elements of planning than the others, these will be briefly outlined and analyzed first. Because the Social Security Act has already been amended several times and since the many details of its functioning are being continuously revised, the description is limited to its major and presumably permanent aspects. (Essential details of its provisions can be obtained from booklets distributed by the Department of Health, Education, and Welfare.)

Public Assistance

Traditionally, public charity was administered primarily on a county basis, usually with States contributing financial support. The public assistance sections of the Social Security Act modified and enlarged such charity programs but did not fundamentally alter their structure. The Act provided Federal grants to assist the States to supply financial help to the aged, the blind, and to dependent children. Originally, the Federal Government matched State expenditures on a 50-50 basis up to $30 per month for old age assistance and aid to the blind, and $16 a case for aid to dependent children. In 1950 the program was extended to include the permanently and totally disabled. The Federal contribution has been repeatedly increased.

Though contributions by the Federal Government did not

change the basic structure of public charity, they have encouraged a large expansion of such programs and they entail considerable expense. In 1937 the Federal contribution to old age assistance was less than $120,000,000; by 1947 it was $472,000,000; and the estimate for 1954 was almost doubled again, at $918,-000,000. Meanwhile State contributions rose from $101,000,000 in 1937 to $617,000,000 in 1953. For aid to dependent children the Federal contribution rose from $12,000,000 in 1937 to $317,-000,000 in 1953, while State funds for this purpose increased from less than thirty million dollars to more than one hundred and ninety million. Contributions at the local level constitute only a small and a decreasing proportion of these programs. Total Federal expenditures for public assistance rose from $421,000,000 in 1946 to an estimated $1,340,000,000 for 1954.

No one can legitimately question that many needy people have been aided by the public assistance program, and that most of these cases have been deserving. At the same time, no one can seriously question that the expansion of the program has contributed to numerous cases of fraud. Partial studies have shown persons receiving relief checks though they are employed; aged parents receiving assistance while living with children financially able to support them; women receiving aid for dependent children whose supposedly missing fathers live in the same home. Another possible adverse moral influence is in the degree to which lenient provisions encourage illegitimacy. (This problem is being solved by no longer recording illegitimate children as such.) The degree that indulgent charity encourages improvidence, illegitimacy and a subtle dissolution of the fibers of character, can only be speculated upon; but one of the economic delusions of public assistance has been revealed in considerable clarity.

Public assistance was first looked upon as a temporary expedient. Charity has always been anathema to visionaries of planned security, and the promise held forth was one which envisioned a marked decrease in the need for charity as other provisions (Unemployment Compensation and Old Age and Survivors Insurance) made their influence felt. Both notions—that Federal contributions to charity would decrease after the depression crisis, and the promise that the other provisions would reduce the need for charity—have proved to be delusions. During the high employment levels of the second world war, and during the prosperous years which followed, contributions went steadily upward instead of down. In the extremely prosperous year of 1953, Federal contributions for aid to dependent children were more than twenty times as high as they were during the depression year of 1937. Meanwhile, unemployment compensation and

Federal pensions had expanded and had been liberalized, far beyond the scope of the original program.

Yet the charity program, instead of withering away under the spreading shade of these growing oaks of security, flourished more vigorously than ever.

Unemployment Compensation

Technically, the sections which comprise the unemployment compensation provisions of the Social Security Act do not constitute a Federal program. The Act provided that a tax of three percent be levied upon wages paid by all employers included under its stipulations, but it left the States free to meet its provisions or to ignore them. Since States which failed to comply would lose large sums each year and receive no benefits, all States soon passed unemployment compensation acts which met the specifications required by the Federal Act.

Use of the Federal taxing power in this manner could be designated as financial persuasion, or as a genteel form of economic blackmail. Money paid to the Federal Government by these contributions of three percent of the payroll is placed in an Unemployment Trust Fund established in the Treasury of the United States. Amounts contributed by each State are recorded in separate accounts and up to 90 percent may be withdrawn as needed. Administrative expenses absorb the remaining ten percent. During periods of low levels of unemployment, reserves accumulate in the trust fund which the States may draw upon when unemployment increases.

Specific requirements and benefit schedules differ from State to State, but they all include three features which are central to the purpose of the program. To be eligible for benefits an applicant must convince a clerk at the Unemployment Compensation Board (a) that he was employed by a company which is included under the provisions of the Act; (b) that he is out of work through no fault of his own; and (c) that he is employable and willing to work. Millions of citizens have found themselves in such circumstances since the passage of the Act, and have benefited by its provisions. By far the majority of these workers have conscientiously met the required standards and received needed assistance in a time of personal crisis. Such beneficial results of the unemployment compensation program should not be forgotten while considering some of its other effects and implications, less obvious and far less known.

Many specific abuses have been revealed in connection with the program. It has been estimated that in some States as high as twenty percent of unemployment compensation funds is paid to persons who fail to meet the stipulated qualifications. Some such payments arise out of misunderstanding, others through fraud. Payments for unemployment compensation come entirely from employers, and many workers do not realize this. Seeing deductions for Social Security on their paychecks, it is assumed that part of their wages are being contributed toward possible unemployment. Some carry the thought a bit further and contend that their contributions entitle them to benefits which they will never collect, especially if they work steadily. Thus unemployment compensation is sometimes conceived as a pre-paid Federal vacation plan! Others seek jobs only in pleasant surroundings, leaving the north during winter to lie on Florida beaches and wait for work to come up over the horizon. Where husband and wife both work it is convenient for the little woman periodically to take time off to catch up with her housework.

Benefits in some States amount to $35 per week. While average weekly wages may be appreciably higher than this amount, several factors make the lesser sum obtained by not working equivalent, or nearly so, to a larger amount earned by working. For example, a stenographer who earns a weekly wage of $50 finds about $10 deducted for Federal taxes, another dollar or so for State or city taxes, and another dollar for Social Security. She has her carfare, lunches, and clothing expenses to deduct. In such cases the differential becomes so small that a period of unemployment is little economic handicap.

It can be protested that these workers fail to qualify, true. And it is in relation to precisely such matters that intangible psychological elements enter the situation.

In theory, the merits of all cases could be carefully examined and all questionable claims rejected. In practice, those who administer the funds are in their sympathies likely to lean toward claimants. Claimants are fellow-workers, and many are filled with self-induced conviction about the justice of their claim no matter how specious the pretext on which it rests. To accede to their request makes the disburser a good fellow, while to reject it may work unwarranted hardship. Rejection may also lead to formal appeals, or to informal political pressures. To illustrate the lengths to which this process of leniency can go, the mother of a child appealed her case after her unemployment compensation had been stopped. She had refused to accept a position on the ground that she did not wish to work later than 5 P.M. In upholding her appeal, the Unemployment Commissioner declared that for her to be required to work until 6 P.M. would nullify the social objectives of the Act, would work at cross-purposes with the national defense program, and would deprive the American home and family of protection to which it was entitled! Thus the program is conducive to malingering in addition to outright fraud.

In terms of cost there seems little doubt that the unemployment compensation program is more expensive than would be a program of direct aid to worthy unemployed persons. Soon after the program began to function we entered into a prosperous period of long duration. During the second world war and the postwar years employment and wages were at levels far higher than were ever believed possible. Employers contributed close to $1,500,-000,000 per year, and from such contributions a trust fund of more than eight billion dollars has been accumulated. Despite the unprecedented prosperity, each year some four to five million persons draw compensation, and the total amount disbursed approaches (and in some years exceeds) a billion dollars.

That this is a prodigious and wasteful program few would deny, yet many would contend that its prodigality and waste, though unfortunate, are warranted by the plan. For the plan envisions an accumulation of huge surpluses during prosperous times so that these will act as a cushion to prevent a serious economic decline. Considering the unusually good economic conditions which have prevailed, and the huge sums contributed, the surplus of some eight billions is not impressive. Yet, you might argue, it is an appreciable amount, and we can use it when we really need it.

And therein lies delusion.

Where is the surplus? The answer is: It is in the Unemployment Trust Fund. It consists of interest-bearing securities of the United States Government; and what could be more secure? But if we encounter conditions of general unemployment, what happens? It seems simple enough to answer this question, too: The States draw upon the surplus in the trust fund, and the trust fund in turn draws upon its interest-bearing securities which are converted by the Treasury of the United States.

One crucial question remains: Where does the Treasury of the United States get the money? In answer to this question you are likely to hear all sorts of statements and contentions about the basic soundness of the United States Government, how we all fail if it fails, and you may even find your patriotism questioned. Beneath all of these fine (but irrelevant) sentiments lie jagged rocks of reality—the Treasury of the United States has a deficit of $275,000,000,000. Within the foreseeable future this deficit promises to grow, rather than to decrease. Do I mean to say that our Government is bankrupt? No; but it is solvent only because of trust, and by virtue of the ability of business and citizens to pay taxes. Part of the indebtedness of the general treasury, to be sure, lies in its obligation to the Unemployment Trust Fund. This condition does not alter the basic situation.

Inescapably, when the time comes to draw upon the trust fund, the Government will have to go further into debt; or it must raise the money through further taxes. That is, it will have to do exactly as it would have to do if no trust fund existed!

This is the reality behind the delusion that we providently and scientifically plan for economic contingencies of the future.

Old Age and Survivors Insurance

YOUR *Social Security*. This is the title of a pamphlet issued by the Bureau of Old Age and Survivors Insurance of the Social Security Administration of the U.S. Department of Health, Education, and Welfare. Under the caption *What It Is*, we find this description:

> Insurance for you and your family, based on your earnings in work covered by the Federal social security law—that is Old-Age and Survivors Insurance.
>
> If you work in employment or self-employment covered by the law, you will make social security tax contributions during your working years to provide an income for yourself and your family in case your earnings are cut off by old age, and for your family in case of your death. . . .
>
> Other members of your family may be entitled to payments based on your social security account, both during your retirement and after your death.
>
> The amount of your monthly old-age insurance payment depends on your earnings in work covered by the law. The payments to other members of your family—to your wife, or to children under 18, for example—are figured from the amount of your old-age insurance benefit.

Under the heading, *The Trust Fund*, we learn that:

> The social security taxes collected by the Bureau of Internal Revenue are deposited in the Federal Old-Age and Survivors Insurance Trust Fund and are used to pay all the benefits and administrative expenses of the program. The reserve portions of the Trust Fund—that is, those portions not required for current disbursement—are invested in interest-bearing United States Government securities.

This official description sounds convincing. Yet Dillard Stokes has described the OASI program in terms very similar to those above; and he hastened to state that when millions of Americans accept such an interpretation, "They take it for granted, they take it for fact—and they are dead wrong. *For every statement* [in his description] *is demonstrably false.*" Perhaps Mr. Stokes' expression, "demonstrably false", is too blunt, but a number of fundamental delusions are conveyed by such descriptions of OASI and they will be described after an outline of some of its principal features.

Old Age and Survivors Insurance sections of the Social Security Act have been repeatedly modified since 1935, and virtually all major modifications involve extensions of the coverage, involve increases in the amount of benefits, and involve greater leniency in meeting requirements. At first, agricultural workers, domestic servants, the self-employed, employees of non-profit organizations (colleges, hospitals and religious organizations), and employees of local, State, or Federal government units were excluded. Gradually such workers have been or are being included under its provisions. By 1952 a total of 109,600,000 account numbers had been issued, and estimates indicated that over fifty million persons contributed during that year alone. Both minimum and maximum benefits have been increased, being $30 and $200 respectively, in 1955. Workers were formerly ineligible for pensions if they continued to earn $15 per month; they may now earn up to $75. Proposals are almost constantly being advanced to further increase benefits and to reduce requirements.

Tax deductions, levied on both the employer and the employee, were at first one percent, and they applied only to annual earnings of $3,000 or less. Then the tax deductions were raised to two percent and applied to earnings up to $4,200. Following the 1950 amendment, the tax will be raised to 3¼ percent by 1970. New proposals would further raise the base on which this tax is levied. Payments to beneficiaries increased from $28,900,000 in 1940 to $1,018,100,000 in 1950. In the few years from 1950 to 1954, benefit payments increased to $3,276,000,000. With further liberalization, wider coverage, and rapidly increasing numbers of people who are 65 years of age or over, the payments will soon amount to five billion dollars per year. This is a colossal program—and it is growing.

Many millions of old people, widows and children have been greatly helped by the OASI program, and the critical analysis which follows is not intended to minimize the humanitarian accomplishments but to bring to light some implications of the program, and to reveal some of the delusions associated with it.

Envisioned in the plan was the prediction that contributions by workers would insure them against dependence upon charity in time of adversity. Thus any appreciable increase in governmental expenditures for social security would be offset by a comparable decrease in expenditures for charity. Not only has this compensating factor failed to operate, but the opposite trend has occurred.

For example, OASI payments for the support of dependent children increased from less than five million dollars in 1940 to an estimated three hundred and eighty-five million in 1953. According to "scientific" planning theory, this tremendous increase in insurance payments would appreciably reduce the amount expended for charitable aid to dependent children. Did it? Regrettably, no. During the same interval, Federal contributions in aid to dependent children increased from twenty-seven million dollars to three hundred and seventeen million. The aged? Did the theory of "scientific" planning give the Nation the results which had been predicted? Again, and regrettably, no. Instead of decreasing, Federal contributions to old-age assistance (as distinct from old-age pension provisions, though also a part of the Social Security Act) increased by over four hundred percent. The projected decrease in charitable need among the aged (which should have occurred as Federal pension payments increased from twenty-one million dollars in 1940 to more than three *billion* at present) failed to materialize.

The delusion that Social Security would reduce or, as some hoped, replace charity is shattered by a reality which shows expenditures for charity hugely increasing as the program expands. This particular delusion is one of the minor mirages, however, and apologists for the program could rationalize its collapse in terms of generally higher costs of living and of increased humanitarianism. Yet verily, if the Lord loveth a cheerful giver and careth not whose money the giver gives, He must clasp such "liberal" donors with His warmest embrace.

The collapse of the delusion that social security would reduce if not replace charity temporarily deflated economic visionaries, but their adeptness at rationalizing failures for their programs has been developed through much exercise. They were helped, here, by the fact that most subscribers were not made aware of this phase of the program, or of its failure.

Even more significant are the delusions about OASI which contributors have been encouraged to develop. One of these cruelly confusing, and false, beliefs which is generally accepted as fact is the supposition that OASI is identical to regular insurance. Millions of pamphlets have been circulated, and numerous other methods have been employed by the Government to lead people to believe that their forced contributions to OASI are identical with premiums which they pay for private insurance; that their social security card is the same thing as an insurance policy. I do not mean to imply that this propagandizing was purposeful, or that it is a plot. My interpretation would be that it arose both from the peculiar zeal that leads visionaries to embellishments which enhance the outlines of the vision, and from the eagerness with which so many people seek security.

As a specific illustration, think of the implications of the very title of the Act—*Social Security*. Such wondrous comfort and assurance are stirred in the breasts of men by this fine phrase that those who question it are understandably considered either to be in favor of insecurity or as meanly unsocial individuals. Thus the program is not simply presented as an economic device, but as a social guarantee. As another specific illustration, note the repetition of the word "insurance" in the description above, a description which was taken from an official bulletin.

The Committee on Ways and Means of the House of Representatives pursued an intensive investigation of the entire social security program, and concluded that OASI differs in several fundamental respects from private insurance policies. Differences exist in relation to:

1. *Issuance of a Contract.* In insurance with private firms, a written contract states the legally binding obligations, and benefits involved. Even the Government issues such contracts with regular insurance, such as the National Service Life Insurance (Veterans' insurance) and War Risk Insurance. OASI is not guaranteed by written contract.

Commenting on this point, the testimony revealed:

> We are presenting this evidence here to show that, while it is freely admitted there was no insurance contract, and of course there can be no insurance without a contract, yet repeatedly over the country with bulletins from the Social Security Agency, with radio speeches, and everything else, the people have been told that they have insurance and they have relied on it. All we want to do here is get all of these facts so the fullest and greatest justice can be done to the American people, both young and old, in the improvement of this situation. *(Part 6, p. 992)*

2. *Benefits,* when earned with private insurance, must be paid. Contributions to OASI do not necessarily guarantee benefits. For example, you are denied a pension which you have "earned" if you continue to earn more than an amount decreed by the Government. This provision is, in a sense at least, a "needs test". Since you must show need by the fact that you earn less than a certain amount, the arrangement to that extent loses its insurance character and assumes the flavor of charity.

3. *Taxation.* Benefits from private insurance contracts are subject to taxation by the Bureau of Internal Revenue. Benefits de-

rived from OASI, like unemployment compensation and relief payments, are not taxable.

4. *Rates*. A private insurance company which frequently altered the rate of premium payments, or the rate of its benefits, would be trusted by few. In the Social Security Act, however, Congress reserves to itself the right to alter, amend or repeal any of its provisions. Alterations and amendments have been numerous and, though most of them have liberalized rather than restricted benefits, the possibility of a reversal or repudiation of policy remains. Payment rates have been appreciably increased— and further increases are inevitable.

5. *Returns*. Though with private life insurance your heirs may collect much more than you contributed, while others who live longer pay added costs to compensate for your "good fortune", benefits are much more nearly proportional to contributions than is the case with OASI. Returns from private annuities and pensions are primarily dependent upon contributions; with OASI, benefits depend primarily on need, and contributions of a few hundred dollars can entitle persons to a pension worth an investment of many thousands. If you leave a widow and three children, their benefits will exceed slightly those of a widow alone, even though you have purchased only one-fourth the amount of "insurance". Though you contribute at the maximum rate, your pension will be practically the same as one received by a person who contributed one-third as much, provided he is married and has a child under 18 when he reaches 65. Throughout the program the element of need outweighs that of contribution, again indicating that the program is more nearly one of charity than it is of insurance.

6. *Compulsion*. Another fundamental difference lies in the fact that private insurance is voluntary, OASI is essentially compulsory. You are free to purchase or not to purchase private insurance. You can determine the amount of coverage and select the type of contract. Should you wish to terminate the contract you are free to do so. With OASI, employers are compelled by law to make contributions and also to deduct contributions from the wages of their employees. There is no choice in amount or type of coverage.

Thus in numerous respects OASI differs from private insurance despite the delusion which has been fostered that the two are identical. Related to the delusion that OASI is an insurance program is a widespread belief that it is a system of planned savings. In the *Analysis of the Social Security System* made by the House Ways and Means Committee, the grounds for this belief are demolished under the caption OASI NOT A SAVINGS PLAN:

.... an elderly person, after paying payroll taxes of $81 can qualify for old-age benefits of $85 a month, worth at the time it starts at say age 65 about $10,400 in present value. If he has a wife also age 65 the benefits become $127.50 a month and have a present value of about $16,000. How is such a plan possible? Obviously by using the contributions of others in the system to pay the benefits.

The essence of the OASI program is this: It is a system under which workers pay taxes (contributions) which to an overwhelming extent are used to pay current benefits, graded in a specific manner to correspond to the average wages of the beneficiaries. In return for these contributions the program contemplates that those now making them will, in due course, receive corresponding benefits later on when they need them; such benefits to be paid out of the then current contributions of the working population of that day. Once the fallacious savings concept is abandoned and the true nature of the program is grasped, then the proposals to putting the program on a sounder basis will be more easily understood.

(Appendix II; pp. 1484-5)

A final delusion is the happy notion that good old Uncle Sam has salted away your contributions into the Old-Age and Survivors Trust Fund.

Literature printed and distributed by the Government describes how the trust fund is kept separate from all other accounts in the U.S. Treasury; how benefit payments and administrative costs of OASI are the only expenditures which may be made from it; how the surplus is invested in interest-bearing obligations of the United States; how this OASI fund has accumulated a surplus of over twenty billion dollars. Such literature again stresses the similarity of the trust fund to bank and insurance company reserve funds. Actually this fund is, in substance, a paper fiction in the same sense as is the Unemployment Compensation Trust Fund. The same reasoning applies when the issue is reduced to the basic question—Where will the Government get the money when expenditures exceed contributions? Interest-bearing securities held by the trust fund will have to be redeemed by the United States Treasury. The Treasury has a debt of 275 billion dollars, a debt which is getting larger. It can redeem such securities only by reducing other Federal expenditures—and there is no present prospect of this—or by increasing the tax burden.

That is, the Government can do exactly what it would do if no hypothetical trust fund existed.

Governmental spokesmen protest that banks and insurance companies operate in the same manner, but wide and basic differences exist. While private life insurance companies do have some of their reserves in Federal securities, the average amount is only 14 percent. The remaining 86 percent is invested primarily in private profit-making concerns. During inflationary periods these investments rise in quoted value as prices go up. Governmental securities do not; relative to the inflated dollars, their value declines. A proper analogy between OASI and private insurance would be to find an insurance company which for many years had spent much more than it took in; which had accumulated a huge debt which it gives no indication of ever paying off; and then to buy your insurance from that company.

In the coming years, as a larger and larger percentage of our senior citizens is eligible for benefits from social security, the hypothetical reserve will have to be drawn upon; and this means that the tax burden on wage-earners will have to be appreciably increased. (Between 1940 and 1950 the number of persons sixty-five years of age and over increased by 37 percent while those in wage-earning ages increased by less than half as much.) We are approaching the time when we will find that the reserve supposedly salted away in a trust fund will have turned to bitter disillusion.

Frantic with depression-fear and inspired by a vision of hope, we embarked upon planned programs—to attain security. From the perspective of the individuals who have profited by such programs, they constitute unalloyed good. From an humanitarian perspective we all derive a warm glow from an awareness that millions of unemployed, aged, children and handicapped have been helped, and for the most part without incurring the sense of shame which goes with charity.

From a political purview these programs have such vote-appeal that few have dared to seriously question them. Economically, they involve tremendous administrative expense which could largely be avoided by direct humanitarian services to meet identical needs. Much additional economic loss arises from the types of fraud and deceit which are encouraged. The economic dream that they would replace charity and provide assurance against depression has proved to have no more substance than other economic dreams. As their expense mounts, the dream of the past becomes a nightmare for the future.

Federal expenditures increased from less than four billion dollars in 1930 to more than seventy-four billion in 1953. The impact on us, each year, increased from $27 to $471 per person. The annual interest on the national debt grew to seven billion dollars. We now pay more than twice our total expenditures for 1930, in interest charges alone. While the bulk of our current expenditures is for military services, a large share of the remainder is for programs similar to those described. When it is protested that to reduce the latter would cut expenditures only by a small percentage, it might be well to paraphrase an old adage: A man who earns $5,000 and spends but $4,900 preserves his solvency and assures his future; a man who earns $5,000 but regularly spends $5,050 is soon bereft of credit.

"Social security" was not derived from the Act of 1935. Nor will any modifications of such legislation retain the quicksilver substance of security within our grasp. Despite delusions which are created to bemuse us, an alleviation of conditions of economic adversity covered by the Act still depends upon faith, hope and charity.

We are compelled to rely upon faith that the Government will not repudiate the promise made to us; since the Government lacks resources of its own, this faith rests upon a hope that taxpayers of the future will be charitable enough to contribute to us as we now contribute to others in their time of need.

In reality we have a choice: To continue to delude ourselves with pretty phrases which cost us mountainous sums in administrative overhead, deceit, and fraud—or to recognize charity for what it is.

Most distressing from a societal perspective is our thoughtless acceptance of delusions fostered by a vision of security; our rejection of the wisdom of the past, and our lack of concern for the future as we grasp in the present its momentary gains.

Chapter IX

The Reality: (*b*) Planned Confusion

Soon after the United States declared war against Germany in 1917, President Wilson appealed to farmers and stressed the need for an abundance of food, not only for ourselves but also for our allies, and not only during the the war but following it. After the Armistice the President exhorted America's farmers to maintain the high levels of production which they had attained during the war, and contended:

> But there is now scarcely less need of increasing the production in food and the necessaries of life. I ask Congress to consider means of encouraging effort along these lines. The importance of doing everything possible to promote production along economical lines, to improve marketing, and to make rural life more attractive and healthful is obvious.

Our farmers responded, as they had responded to the wartime emergency. Their production continued at an extremely high level but meanwhile restrictions on immigration reduced the rate of growth of the American market while the unforeseen rapidity with which European farmers regained their levels of prewar production eliminated the foreign market almost overnight. Large supplies of food were being produced for a market which was seriously contracted. Prices dropped precipitously. Wilson Gee described the situation in his *American Farm Policy:*

> For the same amount of grain which brought the farmer

$2.31 in 1920, he received in 1921 only $1.21, although it cost him as much to produce it. The cotton grower experienced a still more sharp decline, getting only $1.01 in 1921 for a like amount of cotton which brought $2.48 on the markets the year before. Similar declines, though somewhat less in the sharpness of the drop, occurred in the prices of fruit and vegetables, meat animals and poultry products, so that the average price for all groups of agricultural commodities was on the basis of $1.16 in 1921 as compared with $2.05 in 1920. *(Pp. 21-2)*

Encouraged by the President and by others in government, farmers had expanded their holdings to cope with the postwar demand which had been so confidently predicted. Many had borrowed money to acquire more land and equipment. The postwar price declines saw farm indebtedness triple, from some three billion dollars in 1910 to more than nine billion dollars in 1926. Foreclosures became common.

Various measures were taken by the Federal Government to meet this farm crisis, but they were limited in scope and did not constitute social planning. They were economic measures specifically applied to the particular problem. The National Agricultural Conference called by President Harding in 1922, however, proposed one measure which (though not then incorporated into a program) did foreshadow later attempts to apply planning to American agriculture. One of the recommendations of this conference embodied the essence of the parity program which was to be incorporated eleven years later into the Agricultural Adjustment Act of 1933:

.... that the Congress and the President take steps immediately to re-establish a fair exchange value for all farm products with that of all other commodities; ....

At the time, this proposal was not adopted, but in 1929 the Federal Government did attempt to peg farm prices on a small scale, through a revolving fund of $500,000,000 allocated to the Federal Farm Board. Results, from which we should have learned a lesson, were no more successful then than they are now. As described by Wilson Gee, the attempts to artificially support prices merely postponed, and at great cost, the inevitable operation of economic forces:

While undoubtedly there was an immediate benefit to the farmer in better prices, the surpluses withheld became cumulative, helping unduly to depress the market in subsequent seasons. Moreover, such price stabilization operations soon exhausted the resources of the Farm Board, and having proved impractical as a permanent procedure, were discontinued. *(P. 39)*

The Vision of Parity

Earlier attempts of the Federal Government to cope with agricultural crises were essentially efforts to meet a specific economic condition through specific, limited, and direct economic measures. Indirect efforts in the form of price stabilization were attempted in 1929, but on a limited scale, and they were soon abandoned as their enormous expense and inherent fallaciousness became evident.

Visions of planned security may be dimmed, but they are not extinguished by reality. Advocates of planning bided their time.

Then the fear and uncertainty of the depression of the 1930s presented them with the opportunity to incorporate their vision into the remarkable program embodied in the Agricultural Adjustment Act of 1933. A grandiose, heady vision it was, whereby economic planning would raise and keep farm incomes on the same plane as (on a *parity* with) incomes derived from business and industry. This was the central feature of the Act:

> To establish and maintain such balance between the production and consumption of agricultural commodities, and such marketing conditions therefor, as will re-establish prices to farmers at a level that will give agricultural commodities a purchasing power with respect to articles that farmers buy, equivalent to the purchasing power of agricultural commodities in the base period. The base period in the case of all agricultural commodities except tobacco shall be the prewar period, August 1909-July 1914. In the case of tobacco, the base period shall be the postwar period, August 1919-July 1929.

Though veiled by the Act's cumbersome verbiage, the soft hand of governmental "aid" soon exposed its potentiality of clenching itself into an iron fist of dictatorial power. Taxing provisions of the Act equipped the Secretary of Agriculture with virtually unlimited authority to regulate prices for farm products, and the Act itself endowed the President with a privilege to regulate currency so as to manipulate the entire economy. Within a few years the Supreme Court quite properly declared the Act unconstitutional (*The United States v. Butler, et al.* 297 U.S. 1, 1936), emphasizing that

> The power to confer or withhold unlimited benefits is the power to coerce or destroy. If the cotton grower elects not

to receive the benefits, he will receive less for his crops; those who receive payments will be able to undersell him. The result may well be financial ruin. The coercive purpose and intent of the statute is not obscured by the fact that it has not been perfectly successful. . . .

The decision proceeds also to point out that though the Act was designated as an emergency measure to be applied only to prices of agricultural commodities, the principles contained in it could lead to regimentation of the entire economy:

> If the Act before us is a proper exercise of the federal taxing power, evidently the regulation of all industry throughout the United States may be accomplished by similar exercises of the same power. It would be possible to exact money from one branch of an industry and pay it to another branch in every field of activity which lies within the province of the states. The mere threat of such a procedure might well induce the surrender of rights and the compliance with federal regulation as the price of continuance in business.

Permit me to repeat my theme that neither past failures nor legislative fiat extinguishes the vision. Each generation must learn anew to peer behind its glitter, and to expose the spurious substance which lies beneath its shining surface. Neither law nor past experience protects us from the subtlety of its many tempting disguises. Our persistent vulnerability need not give rise to discouragement and dismay, but it should be recognized as the very essence of the challenge—a challenge which we must successively meet, with integrity and with fortitude.

The flaming zeal for a planned agricultural economy was dampened, but it was not extinguished by the Supreme Court's decision of 1936. Almost immediately the smouldering embers burst into a raging conflagration which destroyed more, both in substance and in value, than all the forest fires of our history. This insatiable fire which is fed by our substance is the Agricultural Adjustment Act of 1938.

The Act of 1938 circumvented the unconstitutional features contained in the 1933 Act with a variety of changes in detail, without seriously curtailing the program of scientific agricultural planning which was embodied in it. In the 1938 version, benefits to farmers are granted for soil conservation rather than for not producing; payments come from the general funds of the United States instead of from special taxes, as was specified in the earlier Act; and an appearance of voluntary participation rather than compulsion is obtained by requiring a two-thirds majority before quota restrictions are imposed. As it functions, the Federal agricultural program includes a wide variety of crop loans, price supports, crop insurance and subsidies for export of farm products, in addition to the parity feature. Various agencies operate within the Department of Agriculture to implement this legislation. Among those which are most closely associated with the overall planning program are the Production and Marketing Administration, and the Commodity Credit Corporation.

As described in the *United States Government Organization Manual 1953-1954* the Agricultural Adjustment Act of 1938, together with its amendments,

> . . . authorizes the adjustment of supplies, through acreage allotments, and adjustment of marketings of corn, wheat, cotton, rice, tobacco, peanuts, and long-staple cotton through marketing quotas, whenever supplies are out of line with demand.
>
> Price support is mandatory, in terms of percentages of the parity price, for corn, cotton, wheat, tobacco, rice, peanuts, wool, mohair, tung nuts, honey, and milk and butterfat. For other commodities, support is permissive.
>
> Support is achieved through loans, agreements to purchase, purchases, or, in the case of some commodities, through a combination of these methods.

Price-support operations are financed and controlled by the Commodity Credit Corporation (1933) and administered by the Production and Marketing Administration (1945). To finance its loans and purchases the CCC was capitalized at one hundred million dollars, with an authority to borrow up to $6,750,000,000. The Production and Marketing Administration is responsible, among other things, for acreage allotments and for farm marketing quotas; for price support; for foreign supply and purchase; for school lunch programs; for marketing regulation; and for transportation and warehousing.

Some of these background factors associated with the development of the parity program show how it grew out of a series of agricultural crises, and how the intriguing vision of planned parity persisted, despite previous failure, and surmounted an adverse decision rendered by the Supreme Court of the United States.

The concept of parity involves a belief that incomes of farmers should be maintained on a par with incomes derived from business and industry. Prices for certain farm commodities during the years 1909-1914 are taken as base figures. An average of the prices which farmers received for agricultural commodities during these base-years is then adjusted to bring it into conformity with changes in the cost of products which farmers must buy.

In simplified form: If wheat sold for an average price of $1.00 per bushel during 1909-1914 and farmers' expenses amounted to $1,000 while in 1950 similar expenses cost farmers $2,500, the parity concept requires Government to guarantee that farmers receive $2.50 per bushel for wheat.

For a number of years the support-level has been fixed at 90 percent of parity. Though Congress passed legislation in 1949 to enable the Secretary of Agriculture to adjust the support-level downward in response to over-production of given commodities, this flexible system was not put into effect for several years. Control over excess production is attempted through the mechanism of acreage allotment. If two-thirds of the eligible farmers agree, the Secretary of Agriculture can reduce acreage and fix marketing quotas for crops which are in excess supply. Failure of the required majority to comply results in parity being reduced to 50 percent. Needless to say, compliance is all but automatically assured.

Extent and Costs of Parity

As you read the critical analysis which follows, may I remind you again that a great many people have been helped by the program. My emphasis will be upon the costs, and upon the complexities which resulted as this laudable program gave rise to colossal waste, and created almost indescribable confusion.

Under the powers granted through the Agricultural Adjustment Act of 1938 and its subsequent modifications, the program designed primarily to help needy farmers in periods of crisis grew into a prodigious (and seemingly perennial) monster. As of December 14, 1953, the Government owned outright:

COMMODITY	UNIT	ESTIMATED QUANTITY
Cotton, upland	Bales	235,403
Cotton, linter	Lbs.	545,786,000
Butter	Lbs.	249,629,000
Cheese	Lbs.	251,488,000
Milk, dried	Lbs.	424,227,000
Cottonseed oil, crude, 1953	Lbs.	25,560,000
Cottonseed oil, refined, 1951	Lbs.	85,422,000
Cottonseed oil, refined, 1952	Lbs.	681,460,000
Cottonseed oil, refined, 1953	Lbs.	38,594,000
Linseed oil	Lbs.	108,645,000
Olive oil	Gals.	203,000
Peanuts, farmers' stock	Lbs.	68,232,000
Barley	Bus.	439,000

Beans, dry edible...............	Cwt.	386,000
Corn	Bus.	470,949,000
Flaxseed	Bus.	253,000
Grain, sorghum	Cwt.	33,000
Rye	Bus.	118,000
Seeds, hay and pasture...........	Lbs.	83,760,000
Seeds, winter cover crop..........	Lbs.	34,354,000
Soybeans	Bus.	797,000
Wheat	Bus.	426,769,000
Wool, pulled	Lbs.	6,284,000
Wool, shorn	Lbs.	90,396,000
Resin	Drums	602,435
Tobacco	Lbs.	4,183,000

The cost of these commodities was $2,619,000,000. In addition to this sum, loans outstanding on crops amounted to more than two billion dollars. A large percentage of such loans will not be redeemed, and these crops will be added to the Federal inventory. Purchases during April-June, 1954, included 125,-000,000 pounds of butter, 65,000,000 pounds of cheese and 215,-000,000 pounds of dried milk. On June 30, 1954 the Department of Agriculture held 440 million pounds of butter, 412 million pounds of cheese and 301 million pounds of dried milk. Despite a 20 percent reduction of wheat acreage, a surplus of a billion bushels remained, representing supports of about $2,500,000,000 on this one crop alone.

In 1954, some $6,230,000,000 were tied up in support programs, and the net loss for the first nine months of the fiscal year was given as $187,000,000. Estimated losses by the CCC for 1953 were $681,700,000, and the borrowing capacity of the CCC was increased to $8,500,000,000.

By 1955 the Government had $7,069,277,000 invested in price-support operations, with $4,971,463,000 worth of farm products owned outright and an additional $2,097,814,000 in loans to farmers for products withheld from the market. Loss for the 1955 fiscal year alone amounted to $799,061,464. The storage bill amounted to almost a million dollars a *day*. The borrowing capacity of the CCC was increased to $12,000,000,000—the third multibillion-dollar increase within two years.

Yet this effort at planning is also a failure. Though the Government drastically reduced the acreage allotments for wheat, cotton and corn in 1955, the 1955 crop of wheat *exceeded* that of 1954 by more than 50 million bushels, the corn crop increased by more than 200 million bushels, and the cotton crop exceeded the estimates by 5 million bales!

A favorable delusion of collectivistic social planners was promoted by the British economist, Lord Keynes, a Fabian socialist. The appealing supposition is that the Government, through economic planning, will build up financial reserves during prosperity and prevent economic depression by expending such reserves during periods of adversity. Such theories provided justification for the parity price-support program during the depression of the 1930s. The 1950s, in any reasonable comparison with the past, were years of unprecedented prosperity during which the Government should have accumulated huge financial reserves. Yet we find Federal indebtedness soaring to ever-increasing heights. In relation to this particular program, losses for the two fiscal years 1954 and 1955 *exceeded,* by several hundred million dollars, *those of the preceding eighteen years—including the depression years of the nineteen thirties!*

Even these astronomical figures are misleadingly low. Even they fail to convey the full magnitude of the program because so much of the cost is indirect, or concealed. Some losses are charged to other programs, such as foreign aid and defense. Most crucial of all are indirect costs in the form of increased prices which the public pays for agricultural commodities. Were all of these computable, the costs of the program would be in terms of billions of dollars per year.

Costs are further compounded by bureaucratic confusion. Numerous instances have come to light wherein private corporations leased storage facilities from one agency of the Department of Agriculture (Farm Credit Administration) for a small amount of money and almost immediately sub-leased a fraction of these same facilities to another agency of the Department (Commodity Credit Corporation) for several times the amount of the complete rental.

In 1950 the United States offered for sale to foreign countries 30,000,000 pounds of Mexican canned beef at 5¢ per pound; 50,-000,000 pounds of butter at 15¢ a pound; 25,000,000 pounds of cheese a 7½¢ a pound; and 60,000,000 pounds of dry beans at 2½¢ a pound, in addition to other commodities at virtually giveaway prices. Between 1952 and 1953 more than 250,000,000 bushels of wheat were sold abroad under Federal subsidy at cut-rate prices. Attempting to reduce its stock of hundreds of millions of pounds of butter, sales in the millions of pounds have been made abroad at prices far lower than our own citizens must pay.

Despite such efforts, and in spite of many millions of dollars worth of commodities which are contributed each year to school lunch programs and to welfare agencies, the mountains of surpluses pile up, and costs continue to pyramid. Perhaps a "case study" of an operation which involved one commodity will illustrate the waste and confusion associated with the program in general.

Planned Confusion

During the second world war the Government supported the price of potatoes in order to encourage production. The support-level was fixed at 90 percent of parity (about $2.00 per bushel), and as an added inducement the legislation guaranteed growers that supports would continue for two years after hostilities ceased.

Here again we have the pattern of "planning". Here also the degree of the crisis was grossly exaggerated, for even during the war there was a surplus of potatoes. The Government spent millions of dollars to support the price of potatoes although surpluses, rather than the predicted shortages, piled up. In 1948, Government expenditures for supporting this one crop amounted to $224,000,000. Though the crisis passed (it had been largely fictitious), supports continued for several years. Farmers, taking advantage of governmental largesse, raised potatoes in unprecedented quantities. In thus pursuing their own economic interests at the expense of the Government (meaning at the cost of those who pay taxes and who purchase the supported commodity) farmers illustrated the functioning of one factor which prevents the successful operation of such planning: In any program of this nature a large percentage of people will succumb to a temptation to permit personal gain to outweigh all else.

Faced with tremendous costs and embarrassed by literally mountainous surpluses of potatoes, the Government proceeded to reduce the parity-ratio to 60 percent and compelled potato growers to reduce their acreage if they wished to participate in the program.

Let us examine some of the confusions and paradoxes which arise. Perhaps such paradoxes can be better appreciated if you, the reader, will attempt to view the circumstances from contrasting perspectives. First, imagine what you would do if you were a potato grower, then think of what you would do if you were a governmental official in charge of the program. With some exaggeration to highlight the paradoxes—but based on actual occurrences—the following situations arise.

During the second world war, advertisers and governmental agencies engaged in campaigns to lead us to believe that "the man behind the gun" would win the war; that "the woman behind the man behind the gun" would bring us victory; that purchasing defense bonds would win the war; that the war would be shortened if we drank more milk ("Hidden Hunger Is an Axis Weapon"); that "Lost Milk Bottles Handicap National Defense"; that "Your Waste Paper Can Help Win the War"; and a great deal of similar nonsense. As a farmer, you stretch your imagination a little, and can almost believe that you are growing hand-grenades instead of potatoes. There is also the very real stimulus of governmentally guaranteed high prices. As a potato-grower you respond to the Government's appeal to increase the size of your crop. You grow potatoes as you never did before. The fervor culminates in the huge surpluses of 1948.

As a governmental official you are sensitive to complaints about the huge costs of the program, so you lower the parity-level and insist that growers reduce the acreage which they devote to raising potatoes.

As a farmer you comply with the letter of the law and reduce your acreage but, seeing that even the reduced level of support makes potatoes a profitable crop, you use more fertilizer and cultivate your reduced acreage more intensively. Result, the potato crop in 1949 is even larger than it was in 1948!

Government agents come to your farm and pay you $2.00 per hundred pounds of potatoes. Being already plagued by mountainous surpluses and wishing to avoid the costs of transportation and storage, the agent sells them back to you for one cent per hundred pounds. That is, if you have 100,000 pounds of potatoes for sale, the agent gives you a check for $2,000. Then what happens? Why, you pay him ten dollars—and keep the potatoes! Yes, you agree to use them only to feed livestock or for fertilizer, but after the agent leaves you begin to ponder the situation. After all, they are perfectly good potatoes, and though they will not bring a price of $2.00 on the market it does seem a shame to let them rot; your small amount will not upset the economy of a big country like America, so . . .

As the Federal official in charge of the program you learn that farmers are re-selling potatoes for which they have received governmental price-support. Something must be done before an already scandalous situation becomes worse. Your researchers recommend that dye be poured over potatoes for which the Government has paid. This dye is harmless and the potatoes can still be fed to livestock, but housewives are not likely to purchase purple potatoes even if offered at a bargain price.

As a farmer you watch the governmental agent pour dye over your potatoes. He leaves. You gaze at your large pile of potatoes, and an idea strikes you. You investigate. Sure enough, the dye has covered only the top layer. You uncover the undyed potatoes, load them onto your truck—and off to market you go!

So the dyeing program fails, and the Government moves into the market. As a farmer you are well aware that the Government is offering you a good price for your potatoes. But you also learn that after paying for them they are left to rot. So you carefully separate all of the choice potatoes and sell them on the open market. Since nobody is going to eat the potatoes which the Government pays for, and since the sole basis of payment is weight, you throw in all of the undersized scrub you happen across, and perhaps accidentally a few brown rocks also get mixed in.

But, as the official in charge of the program, agents now report to you that farmers are passing off a great amount of worthless potatoes upon the Government. You call a conference, and the great minds of your fellow-bureaucrats arrive at a solution. Hereafter, to receive the support-price, farmers can transfer only Grade No. 1 potatoes to the Government. Result: The Government's huge rotting piles are now composed of the choicest spuds in the land. Housewives, meanwhile, pay premium prices for second-grade potatoes.

Mountains of government-purchased potatoes pile up all over the landscape of America. If you are a full-fledged, well-trained bureaucrat you will have little objection to this waste of the taxpayers' money, but you remember the scandal which was stirred up under the AAA when the public learned that livestock raisers were being paid by the Government to destroy suckling pigs. You know that there are some voters whose consciences become disturbed at wanton destruction of food. Something must be done; these huge surpluses must at least be removed from sight. You order that potatoes be dehydrated, and stored in the same manner that hundreds of millions of dozens of eggs have been dehydrated and stored. Then it is found that the cost of dehydration is greater than the value of the potatoes themselves. You are forced to abandon the idea.

Frantically you try to halt the growth of this bulky monstrosity. You give potatoes away for school lunch programs, to hospitals, to prisons. On the horizon a ray of light appears. Makers of commercial alcohol might be persuaded to replace their present raw material with potatoes, if they can get potatoes at a low enough price. You offer them potatoes at one-tenth of the price the Government has paid and in addition you agree to pay the freight charges. They agree to purchase millions of pounds, and you sigh with relief as in your mind's eye you finally see some small shrinkage in the mountainous surplus. Then one day an underling timidly brings to your attention an element of the horrible reality which frequently disrupts your plans so beautifully conceived. Immediately, you transfer the upstart to another department. (You learned long since that it is virtually impossible to fire governmental employees.) But the damage is done. You are forced to admit, even to your reluctant self, that your latest scheme is also a failure. Before taking advantage of governmental largesse and using potatoes as a base, manufacturers of commercial alcohol used grain. Grain also is under price-support. When these former grain-buyers switched to potatoes they depressed the market for grain. Result: Governmental surpluses of grain piled up, faster than ever before!

Foreign Aid! Mutual Security! International Friendship! Our Good Neighbors Across the Sea! Let us use our surpluses to build up international goodwill. We can always persuade the public that Slobovians or Xenophobians are starving, and that we will create perpetual friendship by providing them with food to relieve their deprivation.

A bright young man advances this suggestion in a high-level conference. Everyone is enthusiastic. You, as director of the program, beam upon the genius and immediately flip the switch on your "squawk box" to put through a promotion for this intellectual saviour—"A real comer, that young fellow." The conferees exchange backslaps and handshakes as they gloat over the ramifications of THE BIG IDEA. Slogans are suggested: "Food for Freedom"; "Spuds for the Fighters for Democracy"; "Vitamins for Victory"; "Choke Communism with Calories"; "Bury the Bolsheviks with Potatoes"; "Potatoes: Peacetime Hand-Grenades"; "Tuber Diplomacy"; "Spur Them on with Spuds"; and "Kalories to Konfound the Kremlin". Surcharged with bureaucratic brains, released from years of oppressing failure, the conference soars dizzily into the stratosphere. Unanimously, it is decided that the program is a "natural"; it ties in with international goodwill, with "defense against aggression"; it is a "must" in the struggle of freedom-loving nations against the dread threat of communism; "sure-fire" evidence to convince skeptics that we are really one-world. That anyone who questions the program will be labeled "Isolationist", is taken for granted. New York newspapers will bestow their almost sacred blessing, at the very least with an editorial; perhaps a Sunday magazine feature can be written (by a cultist) and presented to its readers as an objective appraisal that "Enlightened Foreign Opinion Applauds Our Bold Approach to Peace."

Then someone (perhaps a nephew of the man who earlier pointed out the fallacy involved in selling potatoes to manufacturers of commercial alcohol) mentions *Mexican canned beef*. Jubilation freezes into frigid silence. The "squawk box" is flipped again, this time to arrange for the transfer of a "negativist" who refuses to be a member of "the team".

Indirect and incomplete accounts indicate that many millions of pounds of Mexican canned beef were our reward for assisting

Mexico—"Our Good Neighbor to the South"—to curtail hoof-and-mouth disease. Hoof-and-mouth disease is a serious and highly contagious malady, and it affects cattle. Much expense over long years enabled us to virtually eliminate this disease in the United States, but since contaminated cattle from Mexico could easily stray across the border, reinfection continued to be a hazard. Officials of the Department of Agriculture, properly concerned over this danger, made an extremely generous offer to the Mexican government. We, the taxpayers of the United States, offered to send teams of veterinarians into Mexico to provide free treatment for cattle infected with hoof-and-mouth disease. In addition, according to news accounts, we offered to pay for any cattle which might have to be destroyed. In making this remarkable gesture of "International Goodwill" we neglected to take into account one important factor: Knowledge that a nation is an easy mark spreads quickly, and becomes a fundamental basis for all negotiations thenceforth.

Without implying disrespect for the Navy (in which I served for several years), in our international relationships we have become the proverbial "drunken sailor". Made dizzy by the unpredictable pitching and rolling of our ship of state on the rough seas of international intrigue, we disembark upon foreign shores. Entranced by exotic scenes we quaff the heady brew of flattery and think of ourselves as muscled men. We are easy prey to the wiles of foreign courtesans who lead us to believe that their avarice is a delicate passion.

Mexico refused our fantastic offer to purge her cattle of hoof-and-mouth disease. She insisted that we guarantee purchase of her surplus stocks of beef. This was the source of millions of pounds of canned Mexican beef which we try to sell at give-away prices to other foreign countries, to promote additional "goodwill". Yet whose the error; theirs, or our own?

Despite a record which shows that disposal abroad only adds to already fabulous costs, we did sell potatoes to foreign countries. If you heard of these arrangements you may have felt a sense of relief that we were getting rid of at least some of our surplus; that even though we were not receiving market prices, at least we were getting something. In addition, we were promoting international goodwill.

In 1950 one such foreign deal disposed of 50,000 tons of potatoes. Price? One cent per hundred pounds. It was reported at the time that each hundred pounds of potatoes was packaged in a bag worth thirty cents, and that the foreign purchasers were more interested in getting the 30-cent bags for one cent than they were in getting the potatoes. American taxpayers, meanwhile, were paying between five and six dollars per hundred pounds.

International goodwill? These 50,000 tons of potatoes were sold to the communists of East Germany.

Costs, chaos and acreage curtailments finally became sufficiently publicized to force the Government to abandon supports for potatoes. But the roots of planning were not destroyed, and they have wormed their way through many niches in the form of supports for a variety of other commodities. Supports for potatoes were again proposed in Congress in 1954, whereupon, according to *Time* magazine, the Wisconsin Potato Growers Association sent this plea to the Secretary of Agriculture:

> Historically, any Government aid to potato prices has led to surpluses, public resentment and lowered per capita consumption. Please do not put the kiss of death on this next potato crop by providing any form of potato price support now.

The brief and chaotic history of price-supports on potatoes is sufficient to indicate the confusion which arises when Government attempts to guarantee security through grandiose economic plans. Though the type of confusion has been indicated, only a hint has been given as to its *extent*. Remember that potatoes are but one of many crops which are under governmental supports, and the confusion which existed in connection with this crop would be multiplied many times over if the entire program were described. Just one additional instance of confusion will be cited, this one involving dried eggs.

Hundreds of millions of pounds of dried eggs were piled up in government warehouses—while we imported dried eggs from Communist China. One fantastic arrangement involved the sale of almost 32,000,000 pounds of dried eggs to Britain. As approximately three dozen eggs make up one pound of dried eggs, the deal involved more than a billion eggs. These eggs, for which our Government had paid approximately $1.25 per pound, were sold to Britain at 22 cents, a total of $7,000,000 thus being involved in the transaction. While even such a loss is better than permitting eggs to rot in warehouses, all is not so simple.

To enable her to pay for the eggs, Britain was "loaned" $3,000,-000 by the Department of Agriculture and another $3,000,000 by the Economic Cooperation Administration. Six million of the seven million dollars, therefore, were provided by American taxpayers. But (you say), at least we get it back, don't we? No, we don't. It is even doubtful that Britain's real interest actually was in acquiring eggs. At that time (1950) Britain's socialist government was desperate for American dollars, which dollars were needed for foreign trade. By this transaction, six million valuable dollars were acquired. In return, we received the equivalent of seven million dollars in foreign exchange—in British trade areas. So the arrangement was not a total loss—except for one item. You see, the exchange value which we received was limited to the purchase of one commodity, Cheddar cheese.

So it cost us $40,000,000 to purchase the eggs, and the $6,000,-000 which we "loaned" to Britain to pay for them. To balance this, we could buy $7,000,000 worth of Cheddar cheese to add to the millions of pounds which the Government already had in storage. At about the same time that we imported this Cheddar cheese we were selling surplus stocks of Cheddar cheese—to Britain—at half-price!

Here it might be well to point out some of the things on which the parity program floundered. The program failed to take into consideration the changes in agricultural economy. Farm production since 1909-1914 has been increased greatly by improved fertilizers, insect control, better bred livestock and poultry, and by a variety of other factors. Mechanization saves labor and encourages large-scale farming to a degree unthought of a few short decades ago. Of the total value of farm products (some 22 billion dollars) recorded in the 1950 census, almost one-half came from large-scale farming operations, operations which constitute only 9 percent of all farms. Since 1949, when the figures for the census were compiled, the process of consolidating and enlarging farming units has occurred at an even faster rate. Some of these large commercial farms are, in effect, producing for Government subsidies rather than for a market.

The parity plan, by its very nature, had to ignore these changes and remain frozen to a view of farming which has long since become a mirage. The program designed to aid small farmers in their time of crisis now functions largely to guarantee high incomes for corporations which control the big operations.

Limitations of Planning

Many factors prevent the successful operation of "scientific" social planning. We lack adequate factual knowledge, and our comprehension of causal factors is woefully limited. Problems cannot be dealt with separately, nor on the assumption that they represent static conditions. Their interrelatedness is coupled with continual change, to prevent us from pinning down one problem at a time. Lacking insight into collective human behavior, we cannot anticipate how people will react. Inescapably, to determine how compliance can be obtained, planning programs must cope with problems of social control. Finally, and inevitably, the desirability of planning rests upon intangible and changing, but vitally significant, values.

Our factual knowledge already is extensive, and it is likely that improved techniques will sometime eliminate this particular obstacle to successful planning. However, we do lack access to reliable and accurate facts which would be needed for successful planning. For years, governmental officials and labor leaders have argued about the extent of unemployment. Though both groups have access to identical data, they do not agree as to their significance. If figures for unemployment are based upon claims for unemployment compensation, a decline could mean that an actual decrease in unemployment has taken place; it also could mean that many workers, though still unemployed, were dropped from the rolls because they had exhausted their benefits.

Census figures on unemployment have differed widely from similar figures compiled by the Bureau of Labor Statistics. Even were agreement reached about the extent of unemployment, economists disagree as to what percentage of unemployment creates a condition which warrants Government programs to provide relief. Trends in the birth-rate, an important barometer for future economic conditions, are similarly subject to dispute.

Only a brief summary is needed to supplement what was said earlier about our ignorance of the factors which cause social events. In respect to unemployment and poverty, we do not yet know the causes of economic depressions. Neither the time of their occurrence, nor their severity, nor their duration can be accurately predicted. We are ignorant of the scientific causes of crime, divorce, suicide, and other undesirable social behavior. Without validated theories on which to base a program, a trial-and-error approach is of necessity entailed.

Lacking validated theory which would enable all competent observers to reach the same interpretation of the facts, business conditions of early 1954 were variously described as constituting "rolling adjustment", "disinflation", "un-boom", "readjustment", "dip", "catching its breath", "deflation", "boom and bust", "recession" and "depression". This wide range of phrases, as the article in which they were compiled pointed out (*Guaranty Survey*, May 6, 1954), indicates the wide diversity of interpretations which can be derived from the selfsame set of facts. Different political and economic perspectives, rather than validated theory or objective fact, determined whether business conditions were optimistically interpreted as "disinflation" or ominously interpreted as "depression".

Our economic problems are inextricably interrelated with each other and with other aspects of our lives. In Britain, to bolster dollar resources for support of their program of security "From the Cradle to the Grave", it became necessary to place heavy taxes upon American cigarettes, thus affecting smoking habits.

Imbalances in production in Britain are described in John Jewkes' *Ordeal by Planning:*

> The principle of joint demand was neglected so that there were cups without saucers, cups without handles, lots of mugs but no vegetable dishes, eggcups galore when there were few eggs, and so on throughout the whole range of domestic appliances.

One reason why the idea of social planning is so popular is this: It implies different goals to different people. Persons sincerely interested in housing see planning as the solution to the problem of inadequate housing; those concerned about food see in planning the solution to dietary problems; those worried about unemployment envision planning as the panacea; those interested in health see in a planned society their optimum obtained. And so it goes. But experience tells us that not all of these can be attained at the same time, if, indeed, they ever can be attained. Therefore the actual planning may concentrate on housing to the neglect, even to the deterioration, of diet; on unemployment at the expense of diversification of skills and interest in jobs so important in the eyes of psychiatrists. Yet if the solution be sought in compromise wherein the planners sacrifice some elements of the utopistic goals, we then return to the status where we were without the planning, but bent over to a lower level as we shoulder the burden of bureaucracy.

Particularly frustrating to planners is the persistence of unpredictable change. Planners glory in the notion that their schemes are progressive, dynamic, and freed from the retarding influences of traditional beliefs. Yet, paradoxically, an essential characteristic of the planning process is an assumption that basic conditions will remain fundamentally the same. Thus the planners for parity are forced to assume (despite overwhelming evidence to the contrary) that agricultural conditions have not changed fundamentally since 1909. Thus the schemes during the depression of the 1930s assumed perpetually high levels of unemployment and stressed the drastic necessity to curtail our productive capacity. Their pseudo-logic was formidable, and they derided all questioners into shamed, self-conscious silence. Yet just as their plans to relieve unemployment began to function we were faced with a shortage of workers, and in a few short years their frantic pleas to curtail production were replaced with equally frantic pleas to expand production.

During the 1930s virtually all articulate intellectuals were firmly convinced that the future was one of perpetual peace. The League of Nations would prevent war. And even if that exalted body failed of its purpose, the horrors of poison gas and airplane bombing (why, some planes carried huge bombs of 100 pounds!) would effectively deter any nation from starting hostilities—therefore we must plan to educate for peace.

We plan to reduce high birth-rates and we suddenly find that we are plunging into a population decline. For many years, planners pleaded for the conservation of coal and oil, and portrayed a dying civilization should we fail to follow their scientific forecasts. We refused to hamstring the economy according to their notions; we used coal and oil at rates which exceeded by far their dire predictions—and now we have excess production of coal, and larger reserves of oil than ever before. If, in years past, we had planned programs similar to those of the present, the Government would still be buying the output of buggy-whip makers, hoop-skirt manufacturers, and subsidizing the artisans who produced Toby mugs and moustache-cups.

Another hazard in attempts to regulate human behavior according to plan lies in the fact that planners cannot foresee the reactions of human nature. In 1918 the Constitution was amended to prohibit the manufacture, sale and transportation of alcoholic beverages, and the purpose was to legislate people into sobriety. Many who previously had never felt strongly about drinking, rebelled. ("Nobody is going to tell me whether I can drink or not!") During the second world war food-rationing was imposed by the Government. Many, many women whose lives were models of propriety and rectitude; women whose righteous indignation would flame to fever-pitch should anyone dare question their patriotism; who would be shocked into stunned silence at the notion that they could possibly commit a crime, responded eagerly to the challenge which the Government imposed. Hoarding became a national game. Matrons were more proud of their cases of stored food; of their surreptitiously acquired steak; of their clandestinely purchased sugar, than they were of their heirlooms.

Innate individual characteristics and differences in people's background and training produce variety in their responses. When wide variety in response is coupled with the necessarily contrasting perspectives between planners and subjects of the plan, paper logic is ripped to shreds.

To cope with diversity in response and with failure to cooperate with the plan, some control over behavior must be exerted. A bureaucracy must be developed to enforce the plan.

At the very heart of the appeal which socialized planning has for so many sincere people is a conviction that the plan will inspire cooperation. By virtue of such voluntary cooperation, it is contended, no coercion will be required to attain the goals envisioned in the plan. Indeed, many visionaries contend that greater freedom than before will emerge from the planning process. Historical precedent, and our own excursions into planning programs, demonstrates that this dream of socialized planning vanishes with the disturbing light of reality. We have but to think of the planned society of Italy under Mussolini; of Germany under Hitler's National Socialist Party; of Russia, Poland, China and the many other socialist people's republics, to refute it.

Even Britain's long traditions of moderation and independence were rapidly breaking down under the planned program designed to provide everyone with security "From the Cradle to the Grave". Among numerous restrictions associated with food rationing, rent control, price control, building control, and wage control were laws determining when you were allowed to turn on the electric lights in your home, and laws which prevented you from installing a shower in your bathroom or a new roof to protect you from the rain.

Ivor Thomas, himself a prominent member of the British Labour (Socialist) Party, describes how he and others became disillusioned with socialist planning as its restrictions increasingly curtailed freedom. Gentle bonds which at first but mildly restrained, grew quickly more exacting and more rigid, to culminate in a law which permitted the Ministry of Labour to force workers to engage in such occupations as it deemed desirable. Of course, this thinly disguised regimentation of labor was not called regimentation; it was presented as the "Control of Engagement Order". Mr. Thomas, in his book *The Socialist Tragedy*, describes its principal provisions:

> . . . . Under this Order men between the ages of 18 and 50 and women between the ages of 18 and 40 may not be engaged except through an employment exchange of the Ministry of Labour, apart from certain exempted occupations. Workers in coal mining and agriculture are not permitted to leave those occupations. Other applicants at an employment exchange are offered jobs that in the Government's view have the highest priority. If an applicant refuses to accept such a job he can in the last resort be directed, and failure to obey the direction can be punished by a fine or imprisonment. Such has been the law in Great Britain since September 1947. It is true that very few persons have been ordered to take up jobs under the order.   *(Pp. 104-5)*

Planning programs have not yet been developed in America to a degree where such rigid control is required. In agriculture, when it became apparent that acreage control could be circumvented by more intensive cultivation, the Government would have had to specify the amount and quality of fertilizer, the distances between rows and the minimum distances between plants in order to prevent further disastrous surpluses. It is now recognized that governmentally imposed acreage restrictions on one commodity commonly result in devoting the excess acreage to grow some other price-supported commodity. Appeals for voluntary cooperation within the spirit of the legislation being met with defiance, it is now proposed that Government impose the next step: Cross-compliance to compel farmers to limit production of *all* price-supported crops in order to obtain support-benefits for any one.

When voluntary cooperation fails to attain results envisioned in the planning process (as invariably it does), the controls which ensue are created and enforced by a governmental bureaucracy. Bureaucracy is an inevitable auxiliary of planning, so some of the general characteristics of a bureaucrat will be described prior to citing specific results of the bureaucratic procedure.

Robert K. Merton analyzed the bureaucratic personality as one resulting from a situation in which rules become ends in themselves while the purpose for which the rules exist is forgotten. Governmental bureaucrats are protected from loss of their jobs by civil service, and their promotions depend not upon superiority or performance but upon length of service. About the only chink in their protective armor of security is evidence that they have violated a rule. Therefore rules become venerated, as ends in themselves. Bureaucrats develop a great capacity for passive resistance against adapting rules to meet specific needs— "See the man in the next office"; "This matter does not come under the purview of this agency". Rules abstractly designed to promote general efficiency turn out to guarantee inefficiency in specific cases which deviate in even minor degree—as most do. Bureaucratic functioning becomes the law of rules, rather than a rule of law. Much bureaucratic *esprit de corps* is derived from a defense of their own interests and attempts to expand their organization so as to augment opportunities for promotion. Such factors lead Merton to describe bureaucrats as persons who have developed a high degree of *trained incapacity*.

Bureaucracy exists in private business, also, and seems to be primarily a function of the size of an organization. In business, however, a pragmatic test of success or failure exists. Its form is profit, or loss. When a business bureaucracy grows to the point where inefficiency exceeds profits, it eliminates itself—it fails. Governments are subject only to the test of re-election, and the bureaucratic organization is insulated even from this test by civil service classification. Administrations come and go, but their bureaucratic organization, it seems, grows on forever, nourished by its own regulations.

An inescapable concomitant of planning is a bureaucracy which—secure in its own position and with its performance subject to no pragmatic test—sustains itself and grows by multiplying regulations which strangle larger and larger segments of the economy. A few illustrations may demonstrate the nature of the process.

In *Ordeal by Planning*, John Jewkes describes many instances of regulations which serve the primary purpose of providing the bureaucratic monster with paper, the nourishment on which it thrives. Among them:

> A market gardener requires a new shaft for a wheelbarrow, a piece of wood costing perhaps ninepence. A license must be applied for from the surveyor of the district council on the appropriate form. The license has to be registered and filed by the district surveyor and then presented to, registered and filed by the timber merchant. A local authority for roads wishes to improve visibility at a dangerous junction by substituting some twenty yards of iron fence for the existing hedge. To obtain permission to do this five enormous forms and nine maps, some of them coloured, have to be prepared and submitted. The despatch of a small shipment of six drums of lubricating oil involves the filling in of forty-six forms, requiring forty-two signatures, not including the customer's invoice or delivery notes.   *(P. 217)*

Professor Jewkes describes another interesting reaction to planning in Britain. In the recovery of the British economy after the second world war, coal was a key product. Recognizing the crucial importance of coal production, the socialist government provided many incentives for coal miners. Other workers easily persuaded themselves that their work was just as difficult and essential as was that of the miners of coal. When special incentives were granted to miners, other groups developed techniques to reduce their production so as to make their own product a crucial bottleneck in the economy!

The weight of bureaucracy in a fully developed socialist state, such as Poland under the communist régime, is portrayed by Czeslaw Milosz in *The Captive Mind*:

> A whole staff of functionaries sits in every factory, counting, writing reports, compiling statistics; the same thing happens on every rung of the state hierarchy, right through to the state wholesale houses and retail stores. If, at last, the article reaches the consumer, it is very expensive; into its cost are counted the salaries of swarms of bureaucrats through whose hands it must pass.   *(P. 196)*

[167]

Dispatches from Moscow cite the official Communist newspaper *Pravda* as reporting that the Soviet Ministry of Agriculture was burying agricultural production in red tape as in eleven months it had issued 3,846 orders, 2,330 circulars, 856,000 letters and 67,300 telegrams. The *Economic Survey of Europe,* published by the United Nations Economic Commission for Europe, stated in 1953 that each Soviet farm submitted approximately 10,000 figures a year to the bureaucrats who compile statistical data. Every step in planting, raising, and harvesting each commodity is governed by minutely detailed regulations. Many other instances of the strangling effects of bureaucracy could be cited.

Let us look at France. To meet the wartime crisis in 1914, France froze housing rentals. In the typical pattern of planning, rents continue frozen more than forty years later; frozen by governmental fiat—and the basis is still the 1914 level. Largely as a result of its program to assure low-cost rentals, the average age of French houses in 1940 was one hundred and ten years, and France has been described as "The country where the slum is king."

Rather than go into the details of planned housing security which led to this condition, let us take just one French housing law and interpret it by first imagining that we are the bureaucrats who draw up the law, and then pretending that we are landlords looking for loopholes in it.

As reported in *Time* magazine, the French housing law of 1948 was designed to impose uniform rental rates throughout the country. According to the law, landlords are required to compute rentals on a basis of three schedules which determine the amounts of "real", of "useful", and of "corrected" floor space. Many factors have to be taken into account to determine the percentage of "real" floor space which can be legally classified as "useful", but let us concentrate our imaginings upon the provisions of the law which determine the computation of what constitutes "corrected" floor space.

As a bureaucrat, you must try to think of things which, in addition to the size of an apartment, should influence the amount of rent charged. An apartment which is bright and cheerful is more desirable than one which is dingy. With bureaucratic thoroughness, you conceive that the view could also add value. A well-lit room merits 100% value in "corrected" space, but "if half of its surface is in the shadow for a substantial part of the day" its value must be reduced to 80%. If the windows overlook a park or "a remarkable panorama", the "corrected" space can be computed at 110%. If prospective tenants can see only a "wide street or a court or a stretch of grass at least 15 meters wide and without obstructions (not counting trees)" the view-coefficient counts for 100%. This provision of the French housing law is an illustration of the bureaucratic mind in legislative operation.

As a bureaucrat, you are about to grant landlords permission to increase their rentals, if the view from their apartment includes the sight of grass. As a landlord, you could comply with this provision by installing a window-box. So, as a bureaucrat, you stipulate that the stretch of grass must be at least 15 meters wide. As a landlord, you might contend that you meet this requirement because there is a bit of grass between the sidewalk and the pavement on both sides of the street—and by lying down it looks like a continuous stretch of grass. So, as a bureaucrat, you must specify "without obstructions". Then it occurs to you that trees might obstruct the view, so you conscientiously specify that they are an exception!

The sunshine component "should be derived from the length of the longest day of the year. . . ." At this point the brilliant bureaucratic brain apprehends that it might rain on the longest day of the year—so the law meticulously specifies "without clouds". Since the law decrees that rentals may be increased if flush toilets are available, you, as a landlord, pick a second-hand or a junked toilet and place it in your apartment without even attaching plumbing—so the law directs that toilets must be "in good working order".

Naturally, landlords and others who are affected in their economic pursuits by similarly detailed regulations soon develop practices which evade the laws. The main purpose in describing such legislation (besides illustrating *bureaucratise*) is to show that though separate items may have some element of rationality, the items in combination may add up to what can only be termed nonsense, though it be precisely delineated nonsense.

This distinction between separate rationality and collective nonsense is overlooked in most planning programs.

Serious obstacles to successful planning are: A lack of reliable data; the absence of validated theories (permitting the biased basis of particular perspectives and interests to interpret conditions); interrelations between problems, and the persistence of unpredictable changes wherein the rigidity of the plan handicaps progress rather than advances it; the diversity of human behavior and the contrasting perspectives from which the particular program is viewed; the difficulty of enforcing planning without complete regimentation; and a tape-worm bureaucracy which devours the sustenance which is supplied to nourish its host. But over and above these factors, important as they are, separately and together, the issue of planning ultimately reduces itself to a question of the relative importance of values.

What *can* be attained through planning is a delusion of security. Inhabitants of socialist-communist countries are probably convinced that they have attained the reality. Propaganda, brainwashing and regimentation are necessarily involved, but it can be done. Economic security, with guaranteed wages, no unemployment, free medical and dental care, assurance of a regular and balanced diet, and public housing, can be obtained by anyone, for that matter. One has only to spend the remainder of one's life in prison.

Values are intangible, but vital, elements in the lives of us all. Besides being intangible, many values have the peculiar property of fading away once they are attained. Children dream gluttonous dreams of what they will do when they reach the topmost peak of life's attainment—when they have enough money to buy as much ice cream and candy as they desire. But by the time they attain such affluence, candy and ice cream do not seem quite so important as they once did. Children yearn for the time when they can stay up as late as they wish, and when that time arrives they complain that the noise of the kids playing outside keeps them awake at night. Young people in love are convinced that marriage will fulfill all their desires. They envision a time when their sweethearts will be free to talk to them all of the time —and they attain it! Usually, though still perhaps desirable, such values lose something of their glister when they are possessed. Once people fought valiantly, and many gave their lives to attain national independence and sovereign political representation. Now large percentages do not even bother to vote.

Another peculiar attribute of values is a perverse quality that is almost mystical. When we concentrate on one value to the exclusion of others, not only is its flavor likely to be diluted when attained, its fruition may actually involve bitter disillusion. Sometimes, or at least so it seems, the very intensity of our search contributes to failure of attainment.

Several years ago a situation occurred which illustrates this perversity in almost allegorical fashion. A father read about a boy who was killed in a traffic accident. Concerned, as are most parents, lest his own children be run over, he resolved that he would do everything within his power to prevent it. He purchased land on top of a mountain, and there he built his home. Only one road led to it, and signs reading "Children at Play" were posted at every turn. Only one possible hazard remained: His children might be run over by a car backing out of the garage. To eliminate even the possibility of this unlikely accident, he arranged to build a turnabout. An unseasonal rain delayed completion. One day he backed his car out and his youngest child ran up to say goodbye to Daddy. The child was instantly killed.

Call it bad luck; describe it as the fickle finger of fate; blame it on the devil; ascribe it to the Will of God; curse, or pray; or (if your intellectualism compels you to conjure a name to obscure reality) designate it as pessimism, negativism, fatalism. But such is the substance of life, and planning does not change it.

Collectively, our values intertwine economic, political, religious, and societal goals. Our quest for security through supposedly scientific planning can be successful. But before we commit ourselves further to its pursuit we should think both long and hard.

Is economic security the ultimate goal? Is it the exception to the rule that values, once attained, lose their visionary appeal?

Can we be sure that commonplace political, religious and individual liberty, when sacrificed on the altar of economic security, will not rekindle themselves—to become the flaming vision of the future?

Part IV

The Recourse

Chapter X

The Recourse: Integrity, and Independence

THOUGH an examination of our past would speedily reveal unsavory conditions which then existed, and further reveal that "prophets of doom" and "purveyors of pessimism"—then as now—proclaimed our dissolution should we fail to heed their exhortations to reform, yet basic differences seem to distinguish the present from those former days.

Challenge has always existed, and presumably it always will. Nor does the past epitomize stainless virtue and farseeing wisdom in contrast to a present of complete corruption, delusion and confusion. Thieves and swindlers, grafters and political schemers, amply contributed to corruption, delusion and confusion in our earlier history; but the extent of crime, perversion, divorce, and virtually all forms of violations is much greater now, and the base of the depravity is much wider.

Personal Pleasure and Collective Security

At some point, difficult as it is to determine, quantitative differences become qualitative. At some juncture, an increase in the number of microorganisms in your body changes you from well to ill; at some point, an increase in white corpuscles ceases to indicate resistance to infection and forebodes serious malady; at some point, a commendable concern in saving for the future becomes niggardly miserliness; at some point, self-pride ceases to add to dignity and becomes mere vanity; and at some point, ordinary mistakes in perspective, and beliefs which are erroneous, become the illusions and delusions of insanity.

As both the numbers and the varieties of individual depravity mount, it may well be that now (without our knowing) we have passed the point where we can shrug off our own immorality as simply a multiple of that of the past. Though there was crime in earlier days, and perversion too, moral violations were recognized as such, being vigorously condemned and punished with justice that was firm. Violators themselves, usually if not always, recognized the evil of their behavior. Not only are such reactions now being appreciably adulterated by maudlin sentimentality, but they are transmuted into almost the opposite. Ever-wider credence is given to beliefs which are completely at variance with those of the past: Society—not criminals, perverts or immoralists—is to blame; understanding sympathy, not moral indignation, is lauded as a proper gauge of public reaction; condescending tolerance for his benighted parents who imposed their frustrations upon him, not remorse for his own misdeeds, is the measure of a criminal's redemption.

Other significant differences contrast immoral acts which occurred in the past with the general conditions of the present.

Earlier education attempted to forestall immorality and criminality by a deep stress upon the development of character. Though verbal bows are now made to law-observance, much of today's education implicitly condones violations of codes by excessive stress on personality-expression. In courses and books relating to preparation for marriage, and now even quite commonly in religious circles too, doctrines of short-term secular pleasure obscure a past concern for spiritual considerations, societal obligations, and farsighted appreciation of long-term earned rewards.

Thus our frantic attempt to emancipate ourselves from moral codes and from traditional rules of conduct differs appreciably from circumstances of the past. As we look back upon a relatively tranquil surface broken only by sporadic disturbance, we may console ourselves, if we wish, by lowering our gaze so that a few madcap wavelets of the past resemble the muddy turbulence about us.

Even as people individually engaged in criminality and immorality in the past, we also were deluded collectively when governmental graft and favoritism were disguised in patriotic sentiments. Yet also in the collective sphere it seems that fundamental differences distinguish current conditions from those of the past. Again a question arises as to when quantitative increases transmute themselves into qualitative issues, a matter so distinctively different.

Federal expenditures increased from less than $4,000,000,000 in 1930 to more than $74,000,000,000 in 1953; annual costs for each member of the society rose from $27 to $471; and annual interest charges alone amounted to almost twice the total governmental expenditures of a few decades ago. Direct taxes to the Federal Government now take more than half the profits of large corporations; and when indirect taxes, higher prices, and Federal, State and local levies are added to income taxes and taxes for social security, individuals already spend almost half their time working for "the government". Never, in the past, were governmental delusion and confusion perpetrated on such a scale, for so long, upon the citizenry. Our attitudes toward government's interference in our lives, and toward acceptance of governmental charity, have undergone a change. The change is marked. Resistance is replaced by apathy, proud independence by mewling pleas for handouts.

Civilizations, even those eaten by the deepest cancers of corruption, do not die in a day. The "prophets of doom" who earlier predicted a dissolution of the society may have been wrong in their timing rather than erroneous in their reasoning.

In some measure the weakening and diffusion of social controls arises from characteristics of urban living and from extremely high rates of internal migration. Such modes of life, with their stress on superficial and material aspects of personality, encourage people to believe that their hope for short-term secular happiness can be fulfilled through emancipation from time-tested traditions and moral codes. Significant factors underlying our frantic quest for economic security through planned programs are the impersonality and the interrelated complexities of the mass-production system, and the fear inspired by the economic depression of the 1930s.

This combination of fear and hope can be a powerful motivating force in leading people to submit to "expert" authority. According to William Reswick it was first used in a conscious and deliberate way by Henry Yagoda, later chief of the Soviet internal security police.

In *I Dreamt Revolution,* Mr. Reswick describes how, during the Bolshevik revolution, Yagoda was assigned to guard more than a hundred Czarist officers with a force of only a dozen men. As the officers prepared to overwhelm Yagoda's small group of guards and break out, he seized the initiative and entered the barn where they were being held. Blatantly he lied and told the officers that they had been sentenced to death:

> . . . That shocked and frightened them and paralyzed their will to act. Then I added casually that there was still

hope for many, perhaps all of them, provided they were willing to help the Cheka with some badly needed information. Neither the fear nor the hope would have been effective alone, but the combination broke their wills.   (P. 94)

Following the extensive Soviet purge trials of the 1930s Yagoda himself was "liquidated" after he had confessed his "treason". Prior to his liquidation he pointed out to Mr. Reswick (then chief of the Associated Press Bureau in Moscow) the scene of his earlier triumph, and declared: "That's where I discovered how to destroy the enemy spiritually while he is in full command of his physical facilities."

Yagoda's "confession", like countless others which followed, was obtained by the very technique which he himself had used.

Since the Cheka was the Communist ministry of internal security, the officers of the Tsar knew that information given to it would be used against the former régime and against their friends. When they even so much as mentally conceded the possibility that they might barter information and become informers in order to save their lives, they had lost their will to resist. In making this concession, even with mental reservations, they lost their character and sacrificed their integrity. They themselves were lost and, by their example, many others were similarly lost.

This technique of employing fear and hope to destroy integrity through self-degradation of character is an integral part of the process whereby victims are persuaded to make abject confessions of crimes they never committed. In our own case it does not operate so drastically, nor is it consciously employed by others to break our will. But to the degree that we temper moral indignation and salve our sense of justice with a feeling that our own misdeeds are thereby lessened, and to the degree that we condone profligate governmental waste and perpetuate delusion with a hope that we may profit thereby, elements of a similar process are present in both our private lives and our public affairs.

Personal hope and collective fear, conjoining to chip away character and to dissipate firmness of resolution, found in questionable theories their seeming warrant. Inspired by the demonstrable success attained through time-tested methods in the study of physical phenomena, a veneration for science lent unearned credence to theories as yet unverified. These were the scientistic theories of human behavior and economic processes, and they now provide a false but impressive pedestal upon which we can remold our lives. They are built around beliefs which have their roots in the quest for personal emancipation and collective security.

Yet the techniques of scientism can be employed to support practically any belief. Nazi Germany used them as proof of racial differences in support of a program of extermination, enslavement and conquest. Communist countries employ them in a wide variety of propagandistic ways.

In America, those who lead us toward the vision were violently opposed to Fascism and Nazism, and their earlier infatuation for Communism cooled when they were forced, perhaps reluctantly, to acknowledge that their dream-girl wore bloody boots instead of a Cinderella's slipper. They lean toward a more gentle, Fabian, socialism and even this they do not openly espouse. The doctrine, cherished by the many sincere visionaries who subscribe to no specific alien creed, needs description in order to complete this interpretation of factors which underlie our present condition.

The doctrine involved is liberalism, and the form it takes at present is scientific liberalism.

Liberalism

Much confusion and misunderstanding are associated with the meaning of the term "liberalism" when it is used to designate political doctrines or to describe beliefs about personal behavior. Professor Thomas P. Neill's *The Rise and Decline of Liberalism* is, to my knowledge, the most thoroughly documented modern analysis of the varied meaning and background of these doctrines which are exerting such profound personal and political influence. Professor Neill's notable book is the principle source of the following description of the historical background of liberalism.

As a designation for a set of political beliefs, the term "Liberalism" was first used in 1811, in Spain. It was adopted by those who supported a new Spanish constitution modeled after the French constitution of 1791. Those who designated themselves as Liberals were anticlerical. Liberalism ". . . . was doctrinaire, as only the Spanish can be doctrinaire, arbitrary, and, paradoxically, quite illiberal." (*P.7*)

Most people who are familiar with the present-day usage of the word "liberalism" believe that liberals are deeply humanitarian; tolerant of personal shortcomings and misdeeds; convinced that all people are equal and should be so treated; much concerned about poverty and slums, and convinced that the Federal Government can and should remedy such conditions; that "liberals" are staunch advocates of Federal legislation to eliminate the evils of unemployment and the dread of economic insecurity associated with illness or old age. These, and beliefs of similar tenor, are felt to be the substance of "liberalism".

It would surprise many, and shock some, were they to learn that during most of the time that this term has been used it designated a set of beliefs which are almost the exact opposite.

With documented detail, Professor Neill describes how liberalism passed through three overlapping phases. In the process, doctrines which had been identified with liberalism during the earlier phases, were replaced by others. Actually, classical Liberalism was so closely associated with capitalism that property rights originally were venerated above practically all else. During this early phase, liberal doctrine held that poverty resulted from natural laws and that attempts to alleviate it were futile if not disastrous. Liberal doctrine has been consistent in regard to its faith in secular progress, but early liberals were sure that progress would be attained by decreasing the influence of government to an absolute minimum, thereby permitting man's innate rationality to create a perfect society.

Especially in relation to business, liberals stressed non-interference by government as a vital necessity. These *laissez-faire* doctrines (which most people have come erroneously to identify with conservatism) prohibited virtually all governmental influence in economic matters. In their extreme form they would have prohibited even governmental attempts to curb dishonest business practices.

Welfare Liberalism, which began to emerge in the early years of the present century, involves doctrines quite contrary to those which Classical Liberalism espoused. Modern liberals scornfully reject the notion that indolence or improvidence is associated with poverty and assume it to be caused solely by social factors.

It is in relation to the proper role of government, however, that the doctrines of liberalism have been completely reversed. Central to the doctrines of earlier liberalism was a firm conviction that governmental interference, especially in economic matters, would strangle social progress. Modern liberals are convinced of an opposite doctrine: That governmental regulation of business and governmentally planned control of vital economic processes is a panacea for most social ills and a *necessity* for social progress.

Liberalism has been markedly consistent, however, in its attempts to derive its doctrines from what seems to be a scientific approach. Professor Neill describes this tendency as it applied to Classical Liberals:

> The Liberal mind—if we may speak of such a thing—grew up in the age of developing science, hostile to the philosophi-

cal or theological approach to life's problems, sympathetic to the method which proved so fruitful in the physical sciences.
...   *(Pp. 18-9)*

Liberalism has also been consistent in its interpretation of motives for human behavior. Whether to be released through a policy of *laissez-faire* or channeled through governmental regulation, a basic and persistent assumption of liberal doctrine has been economic determinism.

In matters of morality, earlier liberals relied upon the "felicific calculus" of Jeremy Bentham. Modern liberals rely upon similar hedonistic dogma resting upon "scientific" studies by Freud and Kinsey. Professor Neill cites as one of the most important sentences of the nineteenth century the statement with which Bentham brought about an entire revolution in ethics, through his contention that goodness is to be assessed solely in terms of personal pleasure; evil by personal pain:

> Nature has placed mankind under the governance of two sovereign masters, *pain* and *pleasure*. It is for them alone to point out what we ought to do, as well as to determine what we shall do. On the one hand the standard of right and wrong, on the other, the chain of causes and effects, are fastened to their throne. They govern us in all we do, in all we say, in all we think.   *(Vol. I, p. 1)*

A cluster of ideas—an ideology—is common to the doctrines of Classical Liberalism of the nineteenth century as well as to those of Welfare Liberalism at present. Liberals venerate change; they have an abiding faith in secular progress. They rely upon "science" to promote their doctrines—despite the fact that this supposedly infallible method has led them to quite opposite conclusions concerning the relationship of government to economic progress. They have also reversed earlier beliefs about man's innate goodness and inherent rationality, substituting modern (psychoanalytic) beliefs about man's innate badness and inherent irrationality.

They are consistent, however, in their determination to discard restrictions. They contended earlier that the goodness could be released by eliminating governmental restrictions; they now maintain that goodness can be uncovered by tearing away societal restrictions. Now, as then, they are confident that rationality will reign as soon as proper educational techniques are applied.

Beneath surface differences which seem to make modern liberalism distinctively different from that of the past, lie fundamental similarities such as these. Most significant of all, in my view, is a persistence in the liberal mentality, of conviction, vision, and formula.

Professor Neill recounts that nineteenth century liberals were convinced that the secrets of human behavior had been revealed to them and that their knowledge would enable them to regulate the social mechanism almost as easily as they adjusted their watches. They were positive that their "laws" were eternally true and that limitless progress would be attained if society would only apply them.

A different set of secrets has now been revealed. An opposite formula is to be applied. And this set of secrets, and this formula, are enshrined by our midcentury liberals who are still quite resolute in their plans, still quite unshakeable in their conviction—and still steadfast in their vision.

Underlying the surface differences is a conviction that their vision of personal happiness and collective security will be attained upon application of a formula. Though the nature of the formula may change—at one time being *laissez-faire*, at another time governmental regulation and planning—a conviction that secular formulas will solve both social and personal problems seems to be the distinctive characteristic of liberalism. It is ever present.

Conservatism

Possibly because there is a growing appreciation that even supposedly scientific conclusions about life in civilized society are affected more by perspective than they are by the techniques which are used to reach them, several books dealing with conservatism have recently been published. Most nearly analogous to Professor Neill's documented analysis of liberalism is Russell Kirk's *The Conservative Mind*.

At least as much confusion and misunderstanding is associated with the meaning and implications of conservatism as is associated with liberalism. People seem to identify conservatism with obstinate resistance to change. Raymond English, in an article titled "Conservatism: The Forbidden Faith", designates such resistance as *instinctive* conservatism. In addition to this widespread usage, the term is commonly identified with *economic* conservatism. Mr. English, with (I suspect) tongue-in-cheek, defines economic conservatism as a ". . . desire to cling to one's economic privileges if one is fortunate enough to have economic privileges."

Though economic conservatives are violent in their opposition to socialism, it could be argued that they are not truly conservative insofar as they may accept, or even endorse, governmental planning programs from which they themselves might profit.

[179]

More important than their narrowness of view or than their inconsistencies is a somewhat paradoxical situation. Extreme economic conservatives espouse doctrines of economic determinism in a manner quite similar to that of the socialists whom they so bitterly oppose.

Extreme economic conservatism is actually the extreme liberalism of bygone days.

The type of conservatism which is the obverse of liberalism is designated by Mr. English as *philosophic* conservatism. Such conservatism is not limited to economics nor confined to politics; it involves a perspective from which life in general is viewed. The *New Dictionary of American Politics* defines this perspective as:

> A reasoned philosophy, associated with the English writer Edmund Burke, directed toward the control of the forces of change in such a way as to conserve the best elements of the past by blending them into an organic unity with new elements in an ever-evolving society. *(P. 89)*

Conservatives respect reason but they also believe (as Mr. English points out) that no individual, no group, not even any particular generation, can grasp the implications of all socially relevant facts; that reasoning should include past experience, religion, and the precepts which are inherent to our traditions.

In *The Case for Conservatism*, Quintin Hogg explains the seeming paradox involved in the conservatives' earlier opposition to *laissez-faire* and their current rejection of socialistic governmental regulation. Mr. Hogg contends that resistance to both of these opposite doctrines is not evidence of inconsistency or fickleness, but a reflection of a continuing conservative adherence to what might be designated as a motto: "Avoid Extremes." He reconciles the apparent inconsistency in this manner:

> Conservatives think that the doctrinaire application of a political theory inevitably involves the statesman in extremes. In fighting Socialism in the twentieth, as they fought Liberalism in the nineteenth century, Conservatives will be found to have changed their front to meet a new danger, but not the ground they are defending. *(P. 53)*

Present opposition to socialism does not mean that conservatives are callously indifferent to suffering, any more than their earlier opposition to liberalistic *laissez-faire* (which decreed that assistance to the poor interfered with "natural law") proved that they hated either nature or law. No one has a monopoly on humanitarianism. Liberals are simply more free with their promises than are conservatives; they are more magnanimous in distributing present earnings of the thrifty and in mortgaging the earnings of posterity; and they are adept at concocting formulas which for a time delude people into believing that charity is justice.

Conservatives temper their humanitarianism with a consideration of costs which penalize those whose diligence or good fortune has enabled them to acquire savings; and with concern lest their heritage to their descendants be the fetters of burdensome debt.

Their humanitarianism is tempered by an awareness that those who receive largesse readily transform gratitude into resentful demands that their "rights" be further expanded. They are fearful that recipients may suffer from atrophy of character; that a crutch temporarily provided for the victims of adversity may lead them to the permanent use of a cane. Their experience (or perhaps it is only an expression of their nature) leads them to distrust formulas and to abhor deception.

In his *Conservatism*, Lord Hugh Cecil expresses the manner in which governmental assistance to the needy fits into conservative philosophy:

> The duty of the State, then, to give assistance to those that suffer may be regarded either as a matter of national charity, or of national gratitude, or as a matter of mere expediency. And on none of the three grounds has Conservatism any reluctance to support the policy. . . . *(P. 179)*

Lord Cecil goes on to indicate that conservatism, however, does oppose programs of state assistance

> . . . if they are made the occasion of establishing the doctrine that every one has a claim on the State in proportion to the services he has rendered to it. . . . *(P. 179)*

No basic element in the philosophy of conservatism conflicts with humanitarianism exemplified by state charity; with gratitude embodied in awards to the deserving for their past contributions to the society; or with expediency expressed in the form of governmental economic action to meet a crisis, such as a depression. Conservatism does resist programs which disguise charity, gratitude, or expediency with phrases such as "social justice", or which masquerade as guarantees of security.

Conservatives feel that concepts such as "social justice" merely paraphrase the socialistic formula: "To each according to his needs." Their contemporary experience and their historical sense compel them to recognize the regimentation which results as the equation is inevitably completed—"From each according to his ability."

[181]

Thus conservatives, *respecting* but not worshipping the past, attempt to confine change within a framework of the highest traditions of the society. Their nature and their experience combine with an historical sense to shape a philosophic perspective which avoids extremes, is skeptical of doctrinaire political and economic formulas whether they emerge from the socialist left or from the extreme right, and which is intellectually honest.

Russell Kirk sums up his study with an outline of traits which characterize a conservative outlook:

> An affirmation of the moral nature of society; a high regard for property rights which are diffused in the form of homes and pensions and private businesses; a suspicion of highly concentrated economic power, whether it emerge in business, in unions, or in government; the preservation of local liberties, and a zealous adherence to the principle of division of power, "for these gone, the Republic goes, and there remains only the General Will of Rousseau." *(Pp. 424-5)*

The role of conservative statesmen in our international relations is defined by Mr. Kirk as one which respects diversities in other societies, and one in which America's highest obligation ". . . is to provide the example of a decent, tranquil, prospering state, a republic just and free, virtuous and permanent."

Integrity, and Independence

It would be a serious mistake to assume that conservatives are good and liberals bad, or to embark upon a campaign to make everybody a conservative. To do the latter would involve an assumption which characterizes liberalism rather than conservatism: That society can be saved by a formula.

In their selection of elements to be preserved from the past, conservatives may make wrong choices, or they may cling overlong to some outmoded belief. In their rejection of novelty and their resistance to rapid change, conservatives may delay or prevent needed innovations. Conservatives may mistake timidity for wise caution; may allow their allegiance to the past to become a mental blindfold which obscures changes which are fundamental; while under a cloak of veneration for tradition they may selfishly promote their own interests.

A balance is needed between those of conservative inclinations and those of liberal convictions. In our present circumstance this balance, if not lost, is in serious jeopardy. Liberalism, aided and abetted by scientism and supplemented with short-term secular humanitarianism, threatens to engulf us and to drown the moderating voice of opposition.

[182]

Liberalism, with its formulas, always had a strong dramatic appeal to politicians and to intellectuals who were in a hurry to solve the problems of society. The transmutation of Classical Liberalism into Welfare Liberalism fused humanitarian appeal to its historical dramatic appeal. Scientism provided further support as it contributed the prestige of true science and supplied effective techniques to conceal deficiencies in the formulas themselves.

In earlier days a balance between liberalism and conservatism was maintained through religious influences, by a rounded philosophical education which instilled in future citizens a skepticism of cheap formulas for happiness, and by the Constitution.

Now, many religious groups support secular liberalistic materialism; mass communication facilities, and life-adjustment education programs which stress facts rather than principles, reduce the weight of education as a balancing factor and in many instances shift its influence to the side of liberalism. Constitutional safeguards against excessive governmental encroachment have been cynically evaded in recent years and are now readily surmounted by the most specious pretexts. It is a serious imbalance, and it seems to be the source of contemporary challenge in America.

Fostered by hope for happiness and fear of economic deprivation, we have succumbed to seductive idealisms incorporated into scientistic liberal programs. Techniques of scientism have been developed to a degree where they effectively blind us to the corruption, delusion, and confusion associated with such programs. Religion, education, and the Constitution—our former safeguards against secular extremism—have lost much of their effectiveness. In appreciable measure our former brakes are now acting as accelerators, to speed our reckless race toward the twin visions of hedonistic happiness and economic security—government guaranteed.

Maintenance of our personal integrity and our collective independence in the face of subtle temptations, is the challenge which confronts us.

Unlike people of the past, we can no longer depend upon traditional external safeguards to impose their restraining pressures upon our impetuous desires. More than ever before we must rely upon personal conviction and internal fortitude to mold our individual lives and to shape a design for the future of our America.

Thus it is a personal challenge. There is no formula which can be applied to meet it.

To meet the challenge successfully is no guarantee either of happiness or of security—though resistance to temptation may enhance your self-respect.

The following suggestions which rephrase and elaborate Mr. Kirk's description of conservatism may be of some help to those who are concerned over the hazards of our present predicament. Perhaps some surcease from corruption, confusion and delusion may be attained if each of us in his personal life, through his daily acts, and in his social and political behavior,

Respects and cherishes tradition; not with blind worship however, nor as an excuse for personal limitations or social defects;

Is proud of our heritage, but not boastful; skeptical of radical innovations, without being blindly obstinate to change;

Reaffirms the moral nature of society in all of its aspects (Shuns expediency and rejects the philosophy that needs of the moment warrant a jettison of principles.);

Reestablishes and reenforces standards of family piety;

When, with lecherous glee, we acclaim the "scientist" who recommends seduction, let us give pause to the thought that his formula will be employed in days to come upon our daughters;

Defends, among other rights of the citizenry, property rights to personal possessions, to homes, incomes, pensions, and to business. When, with jealous envy, we applaud the "statesman" who artfully plunders the resources of the rich, let us give pause to the thought that his wiles, so laudable today, may be directed toward our humbler possessions on the morrow;

Is fearful, and equally, of smothering hugeness, of the universal corruptibility of power—whether it apply to business, to unions, or to Government;

Cherishes high standards of personal conduct, guarding well his independence, and exercising national humility.

Now, in midcentury America, perennial challenge takes a new and elusive form.

So bright is the vision that to some it is a promise which alone lights the way to the future, not a challenge of the present. So deeply immersed within their own affairs are most, that they do not rise to survey a broader scene, to translate their particular twinges of conscience into terms of an epidemic.

So dark is the view to those who stubbornly turn their backs upon all light from the vision that to them their shadow seems a highway back to a lost Utopia.

Those who appreciate the appeal of the vision but find delusion and corruption highlighted by it, are uncertain how to assess its paradoxes.

Not the least of the paradoxes is that the challenge affects all of us—yet must be met by each, alone; that intangibles which vanish under pressure, which vaporize when they are spoken, must be maintained as certainties, solid; that in the present we must fuse the future with the past; that we must convince ourselves that age-old principles are more modern than the latest theory; that the dedication of those who espouse the vision exceeds the depth of conviction of most who oppose it; that in the struggle to swim against the ever-shifting currents of scientism we might be stranded by some wave of the future; that we must encourage education, yet question products of the intellect.

And in all this, we must not close our eyes to the vision, we must profit from any illumination it sheds upon our path.

The challenge lies in shading its incandescence, so that it does not blind us to reality; in reminding ourselves that though brilliance sparks from the wires of the intellect, light's source is from the timeless realistic sun, its reflection from the romantic moon, its consecration from translucent windows of worship.

REFERENCES

CHAPTER I (Pages 14-31)   *References*

Babbitt, Irving   *Democracy and Leadership.* Houghton Mifflin. Boston. 1924 and 1954

Bryce, James   *Modern Democracies.* Macmillan. New York. 1921

MacIver, R. M.   *Society.* Farrar and Rinehart. New York. 1937

Mann, Horace   Twelfth Annual Report, Massachusetts Board of Education, 1849. Cited in Arthur E. Bestor, *Educational Wastelands.* U. of Illinois Press, Champaign, Ill. 1953 *(P. 79)*

Melville, Herman   *The Works of Herman Melville.* Constable. London. 1924. Cited in Erik von Kuehnelt-Leddin, *Liberty or Equality.* The Caxton Printers, Ltd. Caldwell, Idaho. 1952 *(P. 25)*

Perry, Ralph Barton   *Puritanism and Democracy.* Vanguard Press. New York. 1944

Sumner, William Graham   *Folkways.* Ginn & Co. Boston. 1906

Williams, Robin M., Jr.   *American Society.* A. A. Knopf. New York. 1951

U. S. *Government*   *U. S. Government Organization Manual 1953-4.* Government Printing Office. Washington, D. C. 1954

CHAPTER II (Pages 32-50)   *Numbered Citations*

1. (Page 33)
U. S. *Government*
    Communist Activities in the San Francisco Area. House Committee on Un-American Activities. Government Printing Office. Washington, D. C. 1953 *(Part 3)*

2. (Page 35)
Moore, Harry H.
    GANGSTERS, SLUMS, AND DEMAGOGUES IN SECONDARY EDUCATION. *Progressive Education,* Vol. XIII. 1936. *(Pp. 275-81; specific reference, p. 280)*

3. (Page 35)
Butler, Sylvester B.
    WHAT IS EDUCATION FOR CITIZENSHIP? *Progressive Education,* Vol. II. 1925 *(Pp. 210-6; specific reference, p. 210)*

4. (Page 35)
Moos, Elizabeth
    STEPS TOWARD THE AMERICAN DREAM. *Progressive Education,* Vol. IX. 1932 *(Pp. 264-7; specific reference, p. 264)*

5. (Pages 35 and 38)
Shafer, Paul W. and
Snow, John Howland
    The Turning of the Tides. The LONG HOUSE, Inc. New York. 1953 and 1956

6. (Page 36)
Diederich, Paul B.
    WHAT SOCIETY SHOULD BE. *Progressive Education,* Vol. XIII. 1936 *(Pp. 534-7)*

7. (Page 37)
Thomas, Norman
    CAN OUR SCHOOLS FACE FACTS? *Progressive Education,* Vol. IX. 1932 *(Pp. 338-40)*

8. (Page 38)
Laski, Harold J.
    A NEW EDUCATION FOR A NEW AMERICA. *The New Republic.* July 29, 1936 *(P. 343)*

9. (Page 41)
Roper, Elmo
    Collier's. May 12, 1951

CHAPTER II (Pages 32-50) *References*

Chambers, Whittaker   *Witness.* Random House. New York. 1952

Counts, George S.   *Dare the School Build a New Social Order?* John Day Co. New York. 1932

Gehres, Mary Ann   TRENDS IN EDUCATION FOR CITIZENSHIP in *Progressive Education.* (Unpublished)

Hobbs, A. H.   *Social Problems and Scientism.* The Stackpole Co. Harrisburg, Pa. 1953 *(Pp. 161-2)*

Liebman, J. L.   *Peace of Mind.* Simon and Schuster. New York. 1946

Morrison, Charles C.   *Can Protestantism Win America?* Harper and Bros. New York. 1948

Shafer, Paul W. and Snow, John Howland   *The Turning of the Tides.* The LONG HOUSE, Inc. New York. 1953 and 1956

CHAPTER III (Pages 51-65)

Barzun, Jacques   *Darwin, Marx, Wagner.* Little, Brown and Co. Boston. 1941

Benedict, Ruth   *Patterns of Culture.* Houghton Mifflin Co. New York. 1934

Hobbs, A. H.   *Social Problems and Scientism.* The Stackpole Co. Harrisburg, Pa. 1953

Watson, J. B.   *Behaviorism,* and *The Ways of Behaviorism.* Harper and Bros. New York. 1924, and 1928

Woodworth, Robert S.   *Contemporary Schools of Psychology.* Ronald Press. New York. 1948

CHAPTER IV (Pages 66-79)

Babbitt, Irving   *Democracy and Leadership.* Houghton Mifflin Co. New York. 1924

Berkeley, George   *The Works of George Berkeley, D.D.* Edited by G. N. Wright. Thomas Tegg. London. 1843

Ellis, Albert *(Ed.)*   *Sex Life of the American Woman and the Kinsey Report.* Greenberg. New York. 1954

Glueck, Sheldon and Glueck, Eleanor   *Unravelling Juvenile Delinquency.* The Commonwealth Fund. New York. 1950

Kinsey, Alfred C., Pomeroy, Wardell B. and Martin, Clyde E.   *Sexual Behavior in the Human Male.* W. B. Saunders Co. Philadelphia. 1948

———— and Gebhard, Paul H.   *Sexual Behavior in the Human Female.* ————1953

Kirk, Russell   *The Conservative Mind.* Henry Regnery Co. Chicago. 1953 (Edmund Burke to the Chevalier de Rivarol, 1791. Wentworth Woodhouse Papers, Book 1, p. 623)

Orwell, George   *Animal Farm.* Harcourt, Brace and Co. New York. 1947

————   *Nineteen Eighty-Four.* ———— 1949

Sheldon, William H.   *Varieties of Delinquent Youth.* Harper and Bros. New York. 1949

Tocqueville, Alexis de   *Democracy in America.* (Translated by Henry Reeves, Esq.) A. S. Barnes and Co. New York. 1851

CHAPTER V (Pages 80-93)

Asch, Solomon E.	*Social Psychology.* Prentice-Hall. New York. 1952
Babbitt, Irving	*Democracy and Leadership.* Houghton Mifflin Co. New York. 1924, 1954
Cooley, Charles H.	*Human Nature and the Social Order.* Charles Scribners and Sons. New York. 1902
Koffka, K.	*Principles of Gestalt Psychology.* Harcourt, Brace and Co. New York. 1935
Sumner, William G.	*Folkways.* Ginn and Co. Boston. 1906

CHAPTER VI (Pages 94-111)

Egbert, Donald Drew and Persons, Stow *(Eds.)*	*Socialism and American Life.* Princeton University Press. 1952
Huxley, Aldous	BRAVE NEW WORLD, in *"Retrospect": An Omnibus of Aldous Huxley's Books.* Doubleday, Doran and Co. New York. 1933
Jewkes, John	*Ordeal by Planning.* Macmillan and Co. London. 1948
Moley, Raymond	*How to Keep Our Liberty.* A. A. Knopf. New York. 1952
Negley, Glenn and Patrick, J. Max	*The Quest for Utopia.* Henry Schuman. New York. 1952
Orwell, George	*Nineteen Eighty-Four.* Harcourt, Brace and Co. New York. 1949
Schwarzschild, Leopold	*The Red Prussian.* Charles Scribner's Sons. New York. 1947
Tocqueville, Alexis de	*Democracy in America.* A. S. Barnes and Co. New York. 1851
U. S. Government	*Organized Communism in the United States.* House Committee on Un-American Activities. Government Printing Office. Washington, D. C. 1954

CHAPTER VII (Pages 112-128)

Allen, Frederick Lewis	*The Big Change.* Harper and Bros. New York. 1952
Basseches, Nikolaus	*Stalin.* (Translated by E. W. Dickes.) E. P. Dutton and Co. New York. 1953
Beard, Charles A.	*An Economic Interpretation of the Constitution of the United States.* Macmillan. New York. 1913
Chambers, Whittaker	*Witness.* Random House. New York. 1952
Egbert, Donald Drew and Persons, Stow *(Eds.)*	*Socialism and American Life.* Princeton University Press. 1952
Ernst, Morris L. and Loth, David	*Report on the American Communist.* Henry Holt and Co. New York. 1952
Hayek, F. A. *(Ed.)*	*Capitalism and the Historians.* University of Chicago Press. 1954
Hobbs, A. H.	*The Claims of Sociology.* The Stackpole Co. Harrisburg, Pa. 1951
Salvadori, Massimo	*The Rise of Modern Communism.* Henry Holt and Co. New York. 1952

Saveth, Edward N.   WHAT HISTORIANS TEACH ABOUT BUSINESS. *Fortune.* April, 1952

Schumpeter, Joseph A.   *Capitalism, Socialism, and Democracy.* Harper and Bros. New York. (3d edition) 1950

U. S. Government   *Communist Activities Among Professional Groups in the Los Angeles Area.* House Committee on Un-American Activities. Government Printing Office. Washington, D. C. 1952 *(Part III; p. 4092)*

CHAPTER VIII (Pages 129-146)

Stokes, Dillard   DOES OUR SOCIAL SECURITY SYSTEM MAKE SENSE? *Commentary.* June, 1954

U. S. Government   *Analysis of the Social Security System.* Committee on Ways and Means, House of Representatives. Government Printing Office. Washington, D. C. (6 vols., 2 appendices) 1954

CHAPTER IX (Pages 147-171)

Baker, Ray Stannard and Dodd, William Edward *(Eds.)*   *The Public Papers of Woodrow Wilson — War and Peace.* Harper and Bros., New York. 1927 *(Vol. II; p. 433)*

Gee, Wilson   *American Farm Policy.* W. W. Norton Co. New York. 1934

Jewkes, John   *Ordeal by Planning.* Macmillan and Co., Ltd. London. 1948

Merton, Robert K.   BUREAUCRATIC STRUCTURE AND PERSONALITY. *Personality.* A. A. Knopf. New York. (C. Kluckhohn and H. A. Murray, *Eds.)* 1948

Milosz, Czeslaw   *The Captive Mind.* (Translated by Jane Zielonko.) A. A. Knopf. New York. 1953

Thomas, Ivor   *The Socialist Tragedy.* Latimer House. London. 1949

Time magazine   Issues of April 5, 1954 and December 27, 1948

U. S. Government   *United States Government Organization Manual 1953-54.* Government Printing Office. Washington, D. C. 1954

CHAPTER X (Pages 172-185)

Bowring, J. *(Ed.)*   *The Works of Jeremy Bentham.* Edinburgh. 1838-1843. (Cited by Neill below)

Cecil, Lord Hugh   *Conservatism.* Henry Holt and Co. New York. 1912

English, Raymond   CONSERVATISM: THE FORBIDDEN FAITH. *The American Scholar.* 1952 *(Vol. 21, pp. 393-412)*

Hogg, Quintin   *The Case for Conservatism.* Penguin Books. New York. 1947

Kirk, Russell   *The Conservative Mind.* Henry Regnery Co. Chicago, 1953

Neill, Thomas P.   *The Rise and Decline of Liberalism.* Bruce Publishing Co. Milwaukee. 1953

Reswick, William   *I Dreamt Revolution.* Henry Regnery Co. Chicago. 1952

Smith, Edward Conrad and Zurcher, Arnold John *(Eds.)*   *New Dictionary of American Politics.* Barnes and Noble. New York. 1949

[189]

INDEX